Donkey Devos

Listen When God Speaks

ENDORSEMENTS

Who would think that devotions about donkeys could be interesting, much less fascinating, motivational, and spiritually inspiring? But that's exactly what you'll receive as a wonderful gift when you read *Donkey Devos* by Susan K. Stewart. After reading these delightful devotions, I was ready to adopt a donkey and learn valuable lessons about God's ways of revealing his love. But don't worry, we don't have to adopt a donkey to receive the value from this unique book. We only need to read a devotion a day—or two, or three, since I know you, like me, will have a hard time stopping with one. I'm convinced, one (or two) donkey devos a day keeps the heart focused on God and his joy.

—**Kathy Collard Miller**, international speaker and author of more than fifty-five books including *God's Intriguing Questions: 60 New Testament Devotions Revealing Jesus's Nature*

Susan has created relatable and helpful devotions using donkeys, which made me smile. I love the way she shows God's love to us with this unique theme. Her devotions will touch your soul, lift you up, and enrich your life.

—**Molly Jebber**, Amish inspirational historical romance author

In recent years, the concept of the "Dog Whisperer" entered pop culture, encouraging dog lovers to understand their animals, and become "better humans" because of them. In *Donkey Devos*, Susan invites us into the charming world of donkeys—to appreciate and learn from them. Through Susan's insights, anyone can grow in character, and Christ-followers can better bring glory to the Creator who made both people and donkeys.

—**Dawn Wilson**, UpgradewithDawn.com, Heart Choices Today

Hang onto your hats, animal lovers and anyone who enjoys easy reading stories about gentle life lessons. Stewart's *Donkey Devos* are just that. Educational and entertaining, you'll never take the lowly donkey for granted again!

—**Linore Rose Burkard**, award-winning Christian fiction author

Devotionals based on donkeys may sound like an unusual idea, but as author Susan K. Stewart points out, donkeys are mentioned in the Bible more than four hundred times. They are also one of only two animals in Scripture that speak (the serpent being the other). Stewart has taken care of these often misunderstood donkeys for years, and she draws on that experience and on the Bible to create her inspiring *Donkey Devos*. These thought-provoking devotionals will give you a fresh perspective on your spiritual life and on one of God's beloved creatures.

—**Joseph Bentz**, author of *Nothing is Wasted*

Being a city kid, the only time I've had to spend with donkeys has been here in *Donkey Devos*, and believe me, I did not expect the great time I had. These devotions not only showed me that donkeys have gotten a bad rap over the years being called stubborn, but left me with the message that I should remain open to receiving a fresh outlook from God every day. Each donkey devo is delightful!

—Sharon Norris Elliott, author of *A Woman God Can Bless* (Harambee Press) and *Didn't See That Coming: When How They're Living's Not How You Raised Them* (Elk Lake Publishing, Inc.)

Susan's writings have captured the essence of so many facets of what it means to share our lives with donkeys. We share the same appreciation and devotion not only to our donkeys but to all of the wonderful animals in our life.

—Sandy Amy, Zen Donkey Sanctuary, www.zendonkey.org

Susan K. Stewart presents an intriguing premise: that nonverbal animals can communicate with their human cousins, and her book *Donkey Devos* surprised me with how often those cute little equines show up in Scripture. But more so, Stewart artfully weaves in her stories of those cute critters with principles of living, particularly how we can better listen to God's message as transmitted by those "nonverbal" donkeys. And you don't need to be a donkey fan or owner to enjoy the stories and pick up the lessons. Pick up a copy and enjoy it and learn more about how to listen to God's whispers.

—Tim Riter, author of *God, a Motorcycle, and the Open Road*

What can a Christian learn from a donkey? More than you would ever realize! God used a donkey as a messenger in the Bible, and I believe he has used Susan K. Stewart as a messenger too. *Donkey Devos* is about more than communicating with God—it's about being vulnerable so his will can be accomplished; it's about following the guide God has set before us so we can achieve great things; it's about sending up a "bray" to our Almighty God in time of need.

Above all, *Donkey Devos* is a plea to be more like a donkey and way less like a Balaam. A round of applause to Susan Stewart and her actionable advice in a hope-filled book.
—**Shayla Raquel**, Amazon #1 best-selling author

Regardless of your personal opinion about the animals, *Donkey Devos* is a delightful read that pulls from the poignantly simple examples of the country pasture to inspire the reader to see, believe and walk confidently in Truth. Loved it!
—**Katie Hornor**, author, *Faith Like Flamingos: The Christian Business Guide to Walking Out Your Faith in Bold Color*

God still speaks through donkeys. If you doubt it, just read this devotional. Whether you are struggling with loneliness or letting go, change or contentment, or even anger, there is a lesson to be learned from these humble beasts. More than once I found myself giggling over the antics of Jeb, his furry family and friends, and the human ones too. These chapters are short and sweet so perfect for family devotions. We know God loves "all creatures great and small," but there must be a special place in his heart for donkeys
—**Rebecca Kocsis**, General Manager of Christian Home Educators Association of California

Wow, what a fun book! *Donkey Devos: Listen to Your Donkey When God Speaks* is inspirational, heartwarming, and also educational. We all need to learn to "listen to our donkey." Pure enjoyment!
—**Nick Harrison**, author of *Magnificent Prayer, One-Minute Prayers for Those with Cancer,* and *Power in the Promises.*

I freely admit to being a devotional addict. I have been since I learned to read and was given my very own copy of *Open Windows*, in elementary school. I may not have understood it all, but I was excited by the idea of a window looking into what God had to say. Every single day. Since that time, I have always read at least four devotions a day and can't seem to part with any of them at the end of the year.

So I was eager to read something totally different than the hundreds I've finished. Well, donkeys fill that bill, don't they?! And boy did they!

This is one of the most memorable, enjoyable, and insightful devotions I have ever experienced. Susan Stewart reaches deep into the Word and weaves it with such caring, loving lessons involving animals that could easily be "the least of these."

Her lessons are fresh and new. God gifted Susan with an ability to glean incredible learning from mundane things. And he gifted her with an outstanding ability to write clearly, with humor at times and in a manner that made me want to read one after the other. I thought at one point, "This is like potato chips for the brain, I can't read just one."

It was impossible for me to read them without falling in love with Susan, wanting to visit that farm and yes ... consider having a "donk" of my own.

I never realized how formulaic and repetitive devotions can be until I read this one!

Thank you, God, for giving Susan Stewart incredible insight and talent. And nudging her to share!

—**Dr. Deborah McCormick Maxey**, author/artist

Donkey Devos
Listen When God Speaks

Susan K. Stewart

A Christian Company
ElkLakePublishingInc.com

COPYRIGHT NOTICE

Cover and Interior Design: Derinda Babcock

Editor(s): Deb Haggerty

PUBLISHED BY: Elk Lake Publishing, Inc., 35 Dogwood Drive, Plymouth, MA 02360, 2020

Library Cataloging Data

Names: Stewart, Susan K. (Susan K. Stewart)

Donkey Devos: Listen When God Speaks / Susan K. Stewart

120 p. 23cm × 15cm (9in × 6 in.)

Identifiers: ISBN-13: 978-1-64949-155-8 (paperback) | 978-1-64949-156-5 (trade paperback) | 978-1-64949-157-2 (e-book)

Key Words: Devotional Christian; Devo; Inspiration; Animals; Animal devotions; Prayer book; God's amazing creatures

Library of Congress Control Number: 2021933079 Nonfiction

God gave me the gift to teach, and the talent to use the gift through writing. Like so much of life, God didn't give me the power to pen perfect prose. He showed me the path and allowed me to stumble my way to where I'm at now.

Along that path, there have been those who have given me a hand—guiding, teaching, and encouraging. In 2006, I was introduced to a writer who would not only be a mentor and encourager, he would also allow me to call him friend.

Often now as I write, I hear his voice in my ear guiding, sometimes shoving, me in a direction I didn't think could possibly work ... a direction I often didn't want to go. He was determined to pull God's gift and talent out of me.

I dedicate this book to Cecil Murphey because he has continued to believe in me and what God might be able to do through me. Thank you, Cec, for pushing and shoving me along the way. Thank you for your friendship.

TABLE OF CONTENTS

FOREWORD

"I'll get back to you on this. First I need to go talk to my donkeys."

When Susan Stewart was the assistant director for my SoCal Christian Writers' Conference, she sometimes responded to my emails with something like that. Gotta admit, it threw me for a loop at first. I knew she had some donkeys on her property in Texas. But why would she have to pull a Dr. Doolittle before discussing some aspect of the conference with me?

After some time, I figured out that this was her "code" for talking something over with God. She just liked doing that in her donkey pasture. Okay, I can see that. I live in Southern California. I'd love the opportunity to commune with God in a big, lush pasture. (Then again, I have lots of local parks and am just an hour's drive from some beautiful ocean beaches.)

After "talking it over with her donkeys," Susan would respond with wise feedback on the topic in my email. Many times, when we were both unsure of how to proceed in an area, her walk-and-talk with those donkeys resulted in exactly the answer we both needed.

We all have our unique ways of hearing from God.

When I started reading Susan's *Donkey Devos,* I gained fresh insights—not only into why my valued colleague talks to these animals but also how many times donkeys appear in the Bible ... and how God has used them. Along the way, Susan has dispelled the misconceptions I—along with many people—have held about these interesting creatures.

In this book, Susan K. Stewart invites you to take a stroll with her through her pasture. Through these short but insightful chapters, you'll learn more about donkeys than most. And you'll discover nuggets of truth about life that can be gleaned by observing this noble beast ... if you have the right guide. As Susan enlightens you about donkeys and God, you may find yourself eager to go talk to your own "donkeys" for wisdom and divine guidance in the pastures of life.

—**Kathy Ide**, author, editor, writing mentor, conference director, owner of Christian Editor Network

ACKNOWLEDGMENTS

Where does one begin to thank everyone who had a hand in a book? I'm always sure I'll leave someone from the list, then hurt their feelings.

I could, of course, only include the subject of this book—the donkeys in our life. Shawna, Hope, Georgia May, Jeb, and Neesy. I mustn't forget Chuckie, who lives up the road. Then there's the donkeys at Peaceful Valley Donkey Rescue. But that would be silly, right?

Like other writers, I might name all of my writing teachers from elementary school through college. Each one encouraged me and disciplined me with an awful red pen. I've forgotten one or two names along the way, although I do remember Mrs. Turner with her terrible red pen. It wouldn't be fair to name only a few.

Then there're my editors, Jeanne Marie Leach and Deb Haggerty. I especially appreciate they don't use a red pen or red marks.

This book is beautiful because of Derinda Babcock who has an amazing gift of finding the right elements and putting them altogether for the cover and interior of books.

I shouldn't forget the brave beta readers: Dr. Deborah McCormick Maxey, Chris Manion, Cathy Krafve, Mel Hughes, Derinda Babcock, Yvonne Ortega, Kathy Collard Miller, Joel

Comiskey, and Kay DiBianca. These folks helped me keep my fingers on the keyboard by calling me out on errors and urging me forward with this project.

My husband, Bob, is owed my love and appreciation for enduring the hours I spend at my computer writing. He is also the one who stacks the hay to feed our sometimes-obnoxious donkeys.

I sit here racking my brain, knowing someone is missed. I'm thankful to you also, whoever you are.

This devotional began with a glimmer of an idea, which could only come from the Holy Spirit. Without the gifts God has given me, you would not be able to hold this book in your hands. After all God did create the wonderful creatures we call donkeys (and sometimes other not-so-pleasant names). To him, I give all glory.

INTRODUCTION

I became acquainted with donkeys when the Peaceful Valley Donkey Rescue (now located in Texas) opened about five miles from our home in California. I took my grandchildren to see the hundreds of donkeys and other animals housed in the large facility. The creatures amazed me as they never startled or became agitated when strangers entered their area. Most of the time, one would follow or walk beside us as though we were fast friends.

Aware of the social needs of donkeys, Peaceful Valley, doesn't allow the adoption of a single donkey. At the time, we didn't own enough property to adopt a pair of "donks." So, I contented myself with visits.

We had lived on our small bit of Central Texas land a couple of years when an opportunity for a donkey adoption was posted on Facebook. Not one donkey, but five. Three of the jennies (that's a girl donkey) joined us: Shawna, Hope, and Georgia May. The other two moved in across the road. After a few years, our circumstances changed, and the girls moved to a new home. My husband and I visited them and found them quite happy.

A couple years later, Jeb decided to move in. He had lost his original companion, Ellie May. No one knows where she went. She just up and left in the middle of the night. Jeb and Ellie May were from the original five.

We knew he was lonely. Two jacks (that's boy donkeys) in the same pasture isn't always a good combination. Because we didn't want a herd, we knew bringing a jenny over to play might not be a swell idea either. So Jeb lived with the companionship of Pumpkin, one of the barn cats. We knew all along, though, this wasn't the ideal friendship for a donkey.

When our neighbors moved, they needed to find homes for their livestock. We adopted Neesy, a shy little jenny. We moved her ... slowly, but we finished the one-mile trek before the rain started in earnest. We settled Neesy into a smaller pasture until we could take care of the problem with cohabitating donkeys. After Jeb had an eventful surgery, Neesy and Jeb now share the same pasture.

Did you know the Bible mentions three talking animals? All animals communicate with each other. But God decided not to have cross-species chatting. That's why even three animals speaking to humans and being understood is noteworthy.

Each of these creatures had a different message. The first to speak out was the serpent. This character certainly wasn't a model. If God used this snake for a test drive, I can see why he kept the mouths of the other animals closed. This snake in the grass spoke words meant for evil.

In the book of Revelation, John hears an eagle crying "Woe" in a loud voice. A message of warning.

Between these two was the lowly donkey. The beast of burden. This time the animal had words of wisdom. Too often donkeys are mischaracterized as dumb and stubborn. This wrong thinking is what makes the idea of one speaking a message from God so astounding.

Donkeys are mentioned more than four hundred times in the Bible. This is a significant number. Snakes and eagles appear much fewer times. Donkeys are associated with riches and peaceful power. Snakes are associated with evil.

The eagle is considered an unclean animal, but also may represent the strength and greatness of God. Who wouldn't want to pal around with a donkey?

The fact is donkeys are quite smart and certainly aren't stubborn. They've received this bad rap because they exhibit extreme caution. Maybe something we humans should do a little more often. Donkeys won't venture where they aren't sure they're safe from harm. This is how the whole incident for the speaking donkey started.

A quick review: Balaam, the donkey's master, was headed to do something God expressly forbade. God sent a warrior angel with sword drawn to stop the foolish man. The donkey saw the angel; Balaam didn't. The donkey stopped. Balaam beat her and threatened to kill her, until she spoke up. Who's dumb and stubborn now?

Of all the thousands of creatures on earth, God used a donkey to convey his word of wisdom to the foolish Balaam. When Balaam's donkey spoke, he finally listened. (Numbers 22:1–35)

Donkeys are mentioned more than four hundred times in the Bible. This is a significant number. Snakes, or serpents, appear to be less often. Snakes are associated with evil. Donkeys, on the other hand, are associated with riches and peaceful power. Who wouldn't want to pal around with a donkey?

Each day brings a new delight from Jeb and Neesy. I can see them from my kitchen window as they leisurely graze in the pasture or, more likely, stand in the corral looking back at me. They are a constant source of conversation—usually telling us we're not paying them enough attention. Like Balaam's donkey, Jeb and Neesy are never afraid to tell us what they think. They usually think they need more sweet feed grain.

In our years of caring for our donkeys, my husband and I have learned they're also good listeners. Quiet, gentle, and patient. I always have a sense of peace when I'm with my donkeys. When I'm quiet and listen, I can hear God talking to me. Through the antics and travails of life with our donkeys, we've learned much about God and our spiritual lives. When our donkeys talk, we listen.

These devotions are based on "talking" donkeys and their characteristics. Many are based on life with our donkeys.

Life with donkeys has been interesting and educational. In addition to learning more about this species of animal, we've learned to appreciate the "lowly" of God's creation.

With these devotions, I'll share some of the lessons I've learned from our donkey friends, the general world of donkeys, and some of the famous donkeys in history.

HOW I LEARNED TO LOVE DONKEYS

Donkeys aren't usually someone's first choice for a pet and certainly weren't mine. I had believed many of the myths surrounding these animals. Until I met some. Until the day I took my grandchildren to visit the donkey rescue we drove by on the way to our house.

That visit wasn't planned. We'd passed by the corrals of donkeys so often I didn't see them any longer. One day, my granddaughter asked if we could stop. Well, why not? We had the time. After a brief visit to the small information center to learn more about the animals at the rescue ranch, we headed to the large corral.

Donkeys and people were milling about everywhere. This was my first face-to-face meeting with a donkey, so I was a little leery. My two grandchildren, ages seven and four, were ready to charge right in. I held them by the hand up close to my legs. An attendant came over and let me know there was nothing to worry about.

I let go of four-year-old David's hand, and he marched ahead. His head barely reached the belly of most of these beasts. No one, donkey or human, seemed concerned. I followed behind.

Soon I noticed one donkey in particular, because he followed David. This big animal liked my wee grandson.

The two wandered around together for the rest of the visit. That's the moment I knew donkeys are special.

At home later that day, I told my husband I wanted a donkey. He laughed, thinking there was no way I could be serious. I was. I stopped by the rescue a few days later and inquired about adopting. I learned we didn't have enough acreage for two donkeys. And because of their social nature, they didn't allow the adoption of only one. *Sigh*. I resigned myself to the idea I couldn't have a donkey in the backyard.

I'd been like so many of us. My previous opinion of donkeys was based on myth and ignorance. Without ever learning more, I thought they were dumb, mean, and stubborn. Animals to fear.

Oh, how often do we do that exact thing with our fellow humans? We judge based on appearance, lack of information, and the attitudes of others.

Jesus told us to love others as much as we love ourselves (Matthew 22:39). Not only those who look like us or act like us or think like us. In fact, I don't see a qualifier at all. We are to love *all* others.

Has there been someone you thought you couldn't love or even like based on human standards rather than God's, then later found out this person was a joy to know? Through the eyes of love, we can care for anyone, even a dusty, slow-moving donkey.

You shall love your neighbor as yourself.
–Matthew 22:39

THE PEACEABLE KINGDOM

Are you familiar with Edwards Hicks's painting *The Peaceable Kingdom*? What most of us don't know is Hicks painted more than one hundred versions. Each had similar elements like lions, lambs, small children, and William Penn's treaty with Native Americans. Sadly, I can't find a donkey in any of the versions. Probably because donkeys hadn't been introduced to that part of North America in the late eighteenth and early nineteenth centuries.

We unofficially call our little plot of land in Central Texas the "Peaceable Kingdom" because our animals get along as well as those in the painting inspired by Isaiah 11. Our donkeys, chickens, dogs, and cats have, at times, all hung out together in the same yard. Not a large pasture. A small one hundred by sixty-foot yard.

Oh, people were happy to give us warnings about ranch animals cavorting together. The donkeys will kick the dogs. The dogs will kill the chickens. The cats will create havoc all around. So, why do these supposed enemies get along so well at Peaceable Kingdom? Part of the reason is they ignore each other. The cats will lovingly rub the dogs' or donkeys' legs. That's about the extent of contact. The chickens do make way for all the bigger animals to roam, probably a peacekeeping effort.

Maybe it has something to do with our expectations. We knew dogs like to chase chickens, so we introduced them to their feathered yard mates slowly with the expectation they could learn to love each other. Maybe love is too strong a term. At least they tolerate each other.

When the donkeys visit in the yard, we have to be more careful. The dogs want to play and tend to get everyone running around the yard. Not a good thing for any of the creatures involved. We do keep an eye out for frisky activity. For the most part, the donkeys are happy to mow down the grass for us and leave everyone else alone.

If these animals can learn to get along, can we humans? Paul was emphatic about getting along with others in his first letter to the Corinthians. He wanted "there be no divisions among you, but that you be united in the same mind and the same judgment" (1:10).

Like the animals, some of us need to be retrained to see other people not as enemies or competition but as creations of the loving God. In this way, we can become agents of God's Peaceable Kingdom.

The wolf shall dwell with the lamb, and the leopard shall lie down with the young goat, and the calf and the lion and the fattened calf together; and a little child shall lead them.–Isaiah 11:6

DONKEYS–GOD'S MESSENGERS

I spend time reading about donkeys. Anyone surprised? The donkey-care section of my home library started when we adopted our first set. I wanted to know how to care for them properly. Since that time, I've read both informative and silly articles and stories about my long-eared friends.

Recently I came across an article, "Torah Metaphors: The Donkey in the Scripture," by Dror Ben Ami in *The Times of Israel*.[1] Ben Ami has some interesting ideas about how God uses donkeys to teach us lessons. In his article, Ben Ami cites several biblical incidents that seem to suggest donkeys represent messages from God.

Balaam's famous donkey clearly brought communication from God. When Balaam was blinded to the warrior angel, God used the lowly equine to speak truth to him.

King David had his son Solomon ride on the back of the king's donkey to recognize Solomon as the next king. This act also implies the animal represents a means by which enlightenment shall reach the people (1 Kings 1:33). (The word actually used is *mule*.) Solomon asked for and received wisdom from God. According to Ben Ami, the idea of this king riding on the donkey represents God's messenger of wisdom was approaching.

Saul, before he was anointed king, was sent to find his father's donkeys. Saul encountered the priest Samuel while on this search. Samuel anointed Saul God's chosen king of Israel. Again, Ami sees this as a connection between donkeys and communications from God. (1 Sam 9–12).

The message when Jesus entered Jerusalem on a donkey? The Messiah, the Savior is here.

I've been known to say, "I'm going to talk to my donkeys." When I head out to the pasture to stroll with Jeb and Neesy, I'm going out to pray. As I walk through the pasture with them, they are quiet companions. No braying. No fussing. We simply stroll together. I think they sense I'm listening. The trees, flowers, green grass, and calm donkeys are peaceful and open my heart to God. In the quiet place, God can deliver his message to me.

Whether God brings you a message on a donkey or on the wind, listen. Let the quiet of his Spirit surround you. Don't make him send a braying donkey.

Let me hear what God the Lord will speak,
for he will speak peace to his people, to his
saints; but let them not turn back to folly.
—Psalm 85:8

GO TO THE DONKEY

Reading the story of Balaam's donkey brings snickers and giggles from eight- to ten-year-old boys. Whether the lesson is taught in Sunday school or through sharing the story with my sons at home, all boys find something to laugh about.

Perhaps the reactions are because adults and children alike envision Shrek's sidekick, Donkey, a talkative and sometimes annoying equine. Or maybe the idea of a lowly donkey talking to the master is funny. Uncomfortable laughter from adults is because we may be too much like Balaam.

Balaam's donkey relayed a message from God. You see, Balaam was arrogant and doing things his way instead of God's way. God needed to get Balaam's attention. A talking donkey would certainly get mine.

As with all the donkeys of the Bible, this creature has no name. Actually, people began giving names to animals much later in history. Even then only pets were named, not work animals. In this story, she is known only as Balaam's donkey. (Yes, the Bible describes the animal as female.)

As we talked about Balaam's donkey in our home, my sons were eventually able to see this donkey's conversation with Balaam was serious business. They recognized the importance of her role in God's message to Balaam.

As the boys moved into their teen years and started listening to themselves instead of God, Hubby and I would ask them, "What is your donkey telling you?" The idea was to get them to think about what God was saying. Even today, when one of our boys calls with a dilemma, we ask the same question.

Donkeys have long been looked down upon as a lesser member of the equine family. Some people see no value in them, other than as a beast of burden. Isn't it like God to use the lowly to confound the mighty?

Do you listen to a donkey? God may not always use a donkey, but he certainly will use whatever means necessary, unique to us, to get our attention. God wants our attention. If he needs to send a donkey to stop traffic on a busy freeway to talk to you, he'll do it.

We can make things easier on ourselves by quietly going to God, asking him our questions, and listening to what he says. Sometimes this requires sitting calmly to hear. I know most of us don't sit long and rarely silently. But God's message isn't going to show up on our phone, although there are times I wish it would.

Go to your "donkey." Listen when she whispers comfort and direction from God.

But he said, "Blessed rather are those who hear the word of God and keep it!"–Luke 11:28

BALAAM AND THE ANGEL

Numbers 22 tells us the full story of Balaam and his donkey. After years of Sunday School lessons, both listening and teaching, I thought the point of this incident was the miracle of a donkey speaking a human language. Recently, I've dug a little deeper and learned more about the circumstances prompting this animal to speak. Let's first review.

Balaam was a prophet who was sought after for his visions and predictions. But he didn't put the word of God first in his life. Balak, king of Moab, was troubled by all those Israelites roaming in the desert, and he feared losing his kingdom to them. He decided the best thing to do was to get a prophet to curse the Hebrews. Balak chose Balaam.

On Balak's first attempt to entice Balaam, God tells Balaam not to go *and* not to curse Israel. Balaam tells Balak's messengers God won't let him go but fails to mention the not cursing part. Balaam was partially obedient. He omitted the instruction he didn't really agree with.

Balak was not a man to be stopped. He sent a second group of emissaries, appealing not only to Balaam's love of money but also to his pride. Once again, Balaam said he needed to talk to God. We know God had already given his instructions: Don't go. Don't curse.

God let Balaam have his way, but God wasn't happy about it. In fact, Scripture tells us God was angry (Numbers 22:22). Although this time God allowed Balaam to go with Balak's servants, God still forbade cursing Israel. The first thing the next morning, Balaam saddled his now-famous donkey and rode off toward Moab.

God sent an angel to block Balaam on his path to self-destruction. This angel had a sword drawn, ready for battle, ready to stop evil. This wasn't a message of glad tidings or joy. The heavenly creature was bringing warning and was prepared to enforce God's command. The donkey did what any smart being would do: she stopped.

The donkey wasn't being stubborn. True to her nature, the animal was being cautious. Why would anyone want to move forward in the path of one of God's messengers brandishing a sword?

Balaam, determined to move forward with his plans, beat the creature until she spoke.

Are we guilty of not heeding God's instructions? How often do we think partial obedience is fine? Frequently, we, like Balaam, press forward with our plan and presume the blessing of God, failing to heed God's clear warnings. Can you picture God on his throne slapping his forehead, saying, "Didn't I tell her not to do that?"

I'm thankful God chooses not to send a warrior angel to stop me when I'm on a wrong path. I'm sure I would cower as much as that little donkey did. Still, I wonder if I'd be like Balaam and lash out at those who try to warn me to look at the problem? Sometimes, I'm afraid I'm a Balaam failing to listen to God.

God may not send a visible angel, but he does attempt to stop us when we're pushing forward with our ill-conceived, prideful plans. Like Balaam, when we finally listen, we confess and turn back. God can accomplish his clear purpose for us—when we listen and obey, then we get to be part of the grand scheme.

But if you warn the righteous person not to sin, and he does not sin, he shall surely live, because he took warning, and you will have delivered your soul.—Ezekiel 3:21

PUMPKIN MOVES

"Be on the lookout for Pumpkin," I told Peggy. "He got out of his cage last night. I think he may be heading back to your place."

"Oh, don't worry about him," she countered. "He'll be with the donkeys."

When we adopted our first group of donkeys, Pumpkin, a young, orange cat, was part of the deal. He was barely a year old and recovering from injuries he received from some mean dogs.

Cats are known to return to their first home. I've been told they need to be caged or kept inside the house for a couple of weeks, so they know they have a new home. Well, Pumpkin was anything but a house cat. We borrowed a cage for him to stay in. Because the weather was warm, I secured the cage against the house and fixed it so he could get under the house where it was cooler during the day. I only thought the cage secure against the house.

A couple of mornings later, I went out to fill Pumpkin's food and water dishes and found he had managed to push the cage away from the entrance I made for him. He hadn't been here long enough to call the Peaceable Kingdom home. So I called Peggy.

During my conversation with Peggy, I learned this cat

had been raised in the donkey feed shed. He may have even thought of himself as a tiny donkey, and he liked to be with his equine friends. He would find them and hang out with them.

I wasn't as confident. His original home was more than five miles away. I had visions of Pumpkin getting trampled by livestock or eaten by a predator. When I hadn't seen him for a week, I gave up hope of his survival.

The donkeys line up at their feed buckets about sunrise for breakfast. They also tell us in no uncertain terms it's time to eat. We established a routine of feeding them sweet feed grain in the morning, and I walked out to do that chore.

I wasn't paying much attention to the surroundings. A hungry donkey demands full attention. As I put the first scoop of feed in the bucket, I looked up to the trees behind the donkeys. There he was! Pumpkin was sitting on a dirt pile behind his donkeys. He had found his donkeys. He had stayed.

Our lives can change drastically, seemingly overnight as it did for Pumpkin. We tend to run back to what we know and what makes us comfortable. We look to the past for our comfort and security. We don't even think about the potential danger involve.

God never promised us a lifetime of comfort or security. In fact, he's clear we will have trials and adversity (John 16:33). But Jesus has overcome the world. He has gone before us so we have his footsteps to follow, no matter the changes or troubles.

Jesus tells us not to look back (Luke 9:62) We are to look at what he's put before us, even if it's scary or unpleasant. Just like Pumpkin, we can settle into our new circumstances. Pumpkin wasn't sure if he was in a safe place until he found his friends. We may not know what lies ahead, but we can be confident we are in a safe place by being near to Jesus as he guides us forward.

Jesus said to him, "No one who puts his hand to the plow and looks back is fit for the kingdom of God."–Luke 9:62

HALTERING DONKEYS

"Donkeys are mean. I wouldn't have one," a neighbor said emphatically. Having never had a bad experience with donkeys, I asked her what she meant.

"They pick up their babies and throw them."

Huh? I've never seen a donkey foal birthed, but I've never read of this being common behavior.

So many myths about donkeys abound. Meanness is only one. I can understand this thinking when a person learns donkeys are guard animals. Or maybe it's all the pictures of donkeys kicking up their heels at someone. After a little time around these loving creatures, I've come to realize they aren't mean; they are actually compliant.

When Neesy came to live with us, she arrived with a horse halter tied in knots and other attempts to make it fit her. It didn't. The knots rubbed on the side of her head while the halter slid back and forth over her ears. Still, she didn't bite or kick—not mean at all.

I was a little concerned about haltering her myself the first time. Donkeys are known for their memory. Would Neesy remember the uncomfortable contraption on her head and balk?

Not at all. She gave me her usual love rubs, and I was able to easily slide the noose over her nose and fasten it around her ears. Just as our other donkeys have done, no fussing, no biting, no meanness. She wasn't even a little stubborn.

I often think we project our own characteristics on animals. How often do we balk when being restrained in any way? Even when that restraint is for our own good?

God gave us a basic list of rules to follow (The Ten Commandments) all of which control our behavior. Not because he's mean and doesn't want us to have fun. God knows when left to our own ways, we soon end up in trouble.

We halter our donkeys so we can guide them safely from one place to another. Usually, from a pasture in which most of the grass is eaten to a new pasture lush with green food. God puts a halter on us for the same reasons: to guide us gently and safely and to give us what is good.

Teach me to do your will, for you are my God! Let your good Spirit lead me on level ground!–Psalm 143.10

GEORGIA MAY'S INJURY

I don't know much about donkey health. When our first set arrived, the previous owner gave me instructions for monthly worm medicine and how to give an annual West Nile virus shot. That was it. The books I read on donkey care primarily discussed show animals, not animals that lived in a pasture.

The morning Georgia May showed up for breakfast dragging one foot behind her, I had no idea what to do. She ate normally and didn't complain about pain. Obviously, though, something was bothering her. I watched her during the day for signs of her leg either getting worse or improving. No change.

I was fairly sure a visit from the veterinarian was going to be quite expensive, so I called my husband, who was out of state at the time. As I talked about the injury, I felt a little silly worrying about a pasture animal. But when we adopted the three jennies, I felt we took on an obligation to care for them. Hubby and I agreed a doc visit was in order.

Dr. Montgomery came out that afternoon and examined Georgia May's hoof, leg, and hind quarters but saw no visible injury or source of the pain. He gave me a jar of medication and instructed to watch her for a few days. Yep, the vet equivalent of "Take two aspirin and call me in the morning."

In a few days, Georgia May was walking normally. Later, I'd occasionally see her limping. Give her the medicine for a few days, and she was fine. I never learned the cause of her discomfort.

During his visit, Dr. Montgomery talked about how gentle she was. He's always prepared for the unexpected when working with injured large animals. Georgia May allowed him to poke and prod without an attempt to bite or kick.

We also can get cranky when we're injured. Physical injury can cause pain, which isn't pleasant. We want to be left alone. Emotional injury also hurts. Pain we may not even grasp, but causes us to be irritable with others. Like the vet with an injured animal, others are cautious coming near us when we're in pain.

God isn't cautious. Jesus knew the pain we endure. (Isaiah 53:4, Hebrews 2:18). He continues to be with us during our times of hurt. Like the vet with Georgia May, God comes to us to heal us and relieve us of the source of our hurt. Unlike Doc Montgomery, God doesn't need to be cautious because he knows the consequences of our pain.

Yes, we may lash out at God. He's still there. We may hurl verbal stones at him, but he'll stay right besides us. Because he knows. The best part is when it happens again, Jesus remains our healing balm. He is always ready to care for us.

The Lord is near to the brokenhearted and saves the crushed in spirit.—Psalms 34:18

THE GREAT DONKEY CHASE

I don't remember exactly how it happened, but I recall the state of confusion that ensued for about thirty minutes up and down our gravel road. Our three donkeys had gotten out.

These three, Shawna, Hope, and Georgia May, had been with us less than a year. Two members of their herd lived across the road. That may have been the cause of the getaway. The girls wanted to see their friends. Or maybe just "donkey business."

After running out the gate—and donkeys don't run often—they stopped to munch green grass along the side of the road. *This will be easy.* Famous last words when dealing with donkeys. I thought I could calmly walk up to Hope, the leader of the pack, attach the lead to her halter, and start leading her back to the pasture. The plan was for the other two to follow behind her.

The best laid plans, you know. As I closed in on these wayward ladies, they kept moving also, keeping a safe distance from me. Hubby tried to circle around behind them, hoping they'd stop moving along. Nope. Now they darted among the trees across the road. To make matters more difficult, they decided to split up.

Of course, we gave chase. What else could we do? I went in one direction, Hubby in another. I managed to get one of these obnoxious creatures (I wasn't too fond of them at that moment) in a narrow space between a barbed wire fence and a tool shed. Reasoning I could grab her halter and hold her while Hubby went through the gate to retrieve the wayward donkey, I leaned down to reach through the fence. *Gotcha.* Just as I touched the halter, she bolted. I fell forward on my knees. Amazingly, I escaped injury. I was especially thankful my arm didn't get caught in the barbs.

Food. That's the answer. They'll follow their food. I grabbed my large garden wagon, filled it with their favorite hay, and pulled it up the road to entice them to follow me back to the Peaceable Kingdom. Nope. These supposed not-stubborn animals were indeed stubborn. They refused to come near, let alone follow the wagonload of scrumptious food.

Well, I can be stubborn too. *That's it, you obnoxious creatures. Go fend for yourselves.* I grabbed the handle of the wagon and stomped back up the road, through the gate, and to the barn. Not a short walk, and I didn't look back. *You three can just stay out there.*

As I reached the corral, I heard a rustling behind me. Do I need to tell you? Yes, three wayward donkeys. Proudly following me. They certainly were proud of themselves for doing what I believed they should have done thirty minutes ago.

I was thankful the day of the great donkey chase was a weekday. Our neighbors weren't home. No one drove by to see how silly we must have looked.

Don't we often give chase to dilemmas? Not all as dramatic as chasing donkeys around but going after problems with our own brilliant ideas for resolution. We make bargains. We bribe. We go running after solutions. We try to grab the problem and control it.

I can picture God watching us as we chase around our problems with our own solutions. Sometimes, I think I can hear him chuckle. He knows we'll eventually give up when we learn our actions don't always bring the desired results. When we stomp off, leaving the difficult problem behind, he gently brings the answer to us.

"Cease striving," he says. "Quit trying to go it alone. Let me handle it. I know exactly what needs to be done." God waits patiently for us to make our way back to his barn, so he can handle the problem with his perfect solution.

I'm slowly learning not to chase my problems using my own devices. God always gently follows me until I give up and let him take care of me.

Trust in the Lord with all your heart, and do not lean on your own understanding.
–Proverbs 3:5

DON'T BE A BALAAM

I don't choose to be like Balaam. Sometimes I am. I won't listen ... even if my donkeys were to speak English to me. Thinking about my actions, maybe I do make a choice to not listen to God, to go off with my own way of doings things. I tend to get the Cliff Notes of God's plan then try to implement it my way.

OK, God, you want me to be a writer. Here's what I'll do. Step one: Read every book ever written on the subject. Step two: Attend every conference I can afford. Step three: Talk with my friends about the great ideas you have given me.

You get it. I do everything but what God said about his plan. *I want you to be a writer, so go write.*

I fear the unknown. So like Balaam's donkey, I stop. I look for a way out. I may even back up. I certainly can make a lot of nonsensical noise.

I hope you're not seeing yourself in my pattern. It's likely, though. Any number of things can prevent us from following God's lead in his plan for our lives. Pride. Fear. Name an excuse. We've all probably used one.

We don't have to be Balaams. What can we do to not be Balaams?

1. This may seem silly to say: Listen to God. God spoke directly to Balaam. Oh, how many times I've wished to

hear directly from the mouth of God. My goodness, I'd accept an email. I like to think that, unlike Balaam, I would heed God's direction.

2. After hearing God's word, follow his direction. How many times does God speak to us in various ways, but we don't heed? Whether it's one of the big commandments, like don't steal or murder, or a small thing, like don't go to that town, pay attention and do as he says.

3. Follow God's instructions *completely*. Too often we pick the parts we like and ignore the ones we don't. Partial obedience can land us in a mess with only one way out—obeying God fully, which we should have done in the first place.

4. Stay away from the evil influence. When God told Balaam to send Balak's representatives home, he meant what he said. Evil is in this world around us. Once we tell iniquity to leave our domain, we don't have to invite it back.

5. Don't rush in as a fool. Satan knows our weaknesses and uses them against us. Balaam desired money and acclaim. Satan used this desire to get Balaam to do his bidding. He foolishly rushed to satisfy his weakness, without considering the cost.

6. Open our eyes. Balaam was focused on his own gain, not on God's instructions. He certainly wasn't carrying God's message. Balaam could only see what appealed to him: gold and fame. He was blind to anything from God, even a sword-wielding warrior of God.

7. Look for God's messenger. God chooses the way to get his message to us, and he will get his message through to us. Balaam was so set on doing things his way, he didn't see the godly messenger. But the little donkey

did and became the messenger. God uses what we will heed.

8. Stop. Stop what we're doing when we can't go any further. God may be blocking the way even when we can't see the obstacle. Instead of pushing forward, stop, rethink, pause, pray. This is a good time to rest and seek God.

Sometimes God uses something inconsequential, like a meek little donkey, to get our attention. When God opens the mouth of our donkey, he is speaking. We need to listen.

Then the Lord opened the mouth of the donkey, and she said ...–Numbers 22:28

GUARD DONKEY

In Texas, and I imagine elsewhere, seeing a donkey grazing in the cow herd isn't unusual. Although donkeys are friendly creatures and enjoy the company of their bovine friends, they aren't in the herd for social reasons. The ranchers allow donkeys because they're good guards.

I wouldn't be surprised if the guard donkeys consider the cattle more than friends, but rather family. Because donkeys like companionship, they become attached to those they spend time with. Of course, they want to protect their family.

People say donkeys are good guards because they have a natural aversion to canines, thus will chase off coyotes, wolves, or wild dogs. I'm not sure about the "natural" aversion. We've had our dogs and donkeys in the same yard with no problems. I do know our donkeys will become nervous and alert us when the coyotes howl.

Donkeys are territorial and defend their home when a predator comes into the area. Although they mix with any herd well, when a newcomer comes into the pasture, the donkey wants to know what's going on.

Jeb has no specific herd to protect, but he does protect his corner of Peaceable Kingdom. The primary pasture is near the front gate. When a vehicle is coming into the driveway, Jeb makes his way to the gate and signals with loud braying someone is coming. Sometimes I'm sure he's hoping the someone is a delivery driver who will leave the boxes on his side of the gate so he can make a snack of the cardboard boxes.

Why donkeys rather than dogs for protection? They mix with the herd. They are less prone to wander off. Plus, they live longer.

Not all donkeys are good at guarding. A jenny with a foal is the best choice when possible. Her natural mothering instincts lead her to be a more alert protector. A john (a gelding) is less aggressive than a jack (intact male) and will mix with the herd well. Jacks are the least desirable because they may also be aggressive with those they are to protect. You know, boys will be boys.

A rancher should know his guard animal well. It's more than the proverbial guardian angel.

Solomon tells us in Proverbs 4:23 to guard our hearts. Psalm 121:5 tells us God is our guardian (MEV). And he protects us from all evil (v. 7). What better protector could we have than the ultimate guardian of the universe?

We need to put our guard donkey in our herd daily. God is part of our lives just as a guard donkey is part of the cattle herd. He knows the predators in our lives, just as the donkey knows the predators of the cows. If we let God roam our pasture, he will protect us. Like the rancher, we need to know our guardian and make him a daily part of our lives.

Be strong and courageous. Do not fear or be in dread of them, for it is the Lord your God who goes with you. He will not leave you or forsake you.–Deuteronomy 31:6

JEB TALKING TO THE GIRLS

Hope, Shawna, and Georgia May were our first trio of donkeys. We adopted these jennies from a camp for children with special needs, which was closing. Jeb and Ellie May, other donkeys from the group, went to our neighbors across the road.

Separating from family and friends is hard for us. Well, it's difficult for donkeys also. These five had been raised together. Jeb was a brother to one of our girls. They were family.

We wondered if they would attempt to have a family reunion. To our knowledge, an escape plan was never hatched. I'm convinced, though, they stayed in touch, much as we do when we move away from those we've become comfortable with.

At the time, several donkeys lived in our little neighborhood. Each morning we heard them calling around to check up on each other. A bray from the south. A heehaw from the east. Our girls raised their voices together, but never in unison. And, of course, Jeb and Ellie May joined in with the donkey grapevine.

For these donkeys who were raised together, the conversation didn't stop with the morning news. Often throughout the day, one of the donkeys across the road called out, and one of our girls replied. In the evening, when we fed the trio on our side of the road, they'd come ambling, announcing to all who listened they were about to be served sweet feed ... Jeb and Ellie May responded. The evening conversation began.

None of the other neighborhood donkeys joined during this time. I'd like to think they knew this was a family affair. They seemed to know this group needed to share with one another because they missed each other. Like sending text messages to our loved ones across the country to check up on them.

Donkeys are loyal. They become attached to those who are around them—animal or human. They enjoy the interaction and miss each other when separated.

Don't we miss our friends and family when we're apart? More importantly, don't we miss God when we feel as though we're separated from him?

God doesn't separate himself from us. Usually, we don't consciously remove ourselves from him. Like the five donkeys from the camp, our circumstances often disconnect us from God. Something major happens in our lives. We forget God in the busyness of life.

Unlike the five equines who had no control over their group splitting, we do. They couldn't change their situation. They lived in two different locations. God, on the other hand, is with us, always on our side of the road. We need only call, then listen.

To summarize a Carole King song: You call, I'll come. God comes. Never fail. We may not always sense his presence, but he's there. Always there. Like the donkey family wanted to hear from each other, God wants to hear us call to him.

Send up a bray and he will respond.

The Lord is near to all who call on him.
—Psalms 145:18

THE SINGING DONKEY

Bray is what we call the familiar "hee-haw" of donkeys. This cry is made by inhaling, then exhaling. "Hee" in. "Haw" out.

Merriam-Webster Unabridged Dictionary calls it "loud *and* harsh" (italic mine). The loud part is definitely true. Once, nearly a dozen donkeys lived in our area. We could hear them talking to each other, even though some were about a mile away. The only louder animal noise is a rooster. The Peaceable Kingdom has both. Can you imagine the greetings we get in the morning?

I take issue with "harsh". The *Cambridge English Dictionary* says bray is an unpleasant sound. At least Vocabulary.com associates the term with laughter or expressing of joy. Like human voices, donkeys have their own voice. Each one can be different and even melodious.

The first time most people heard Georgia May bray, they'd turn to figure out where the "song" was coming from. One time when her vet was leaving, she sang a farewell to him. He'd never heard quite a sound from a donkey. Dr. Montgomery's first reactions was "What's wrong?"

Georgia May doesn't speak with the usual hee-haw. She sings one note. Something like her "hee" gets stuck and she can't "haw." The song is fun to hear. People definitely know when she was talking, and they always seemed to listen.

She's now known in our neighborhood as the singing donkey. I've been asked if I trained her to greet people in such a fashion. No, her one-note melody is natural.

I don't think I've ever heard another donkey vocalize quite like Georgia May does. Sometimes her song is quite lengthy—primarily when feeding time comes around, and I'm not getting to the feed bucket as fast as she thinks I should. Other times when we're conversing, her song is shorter and quieter. There's a sense of contentment in her voice.

Don't we often sing or hum when we're happy and at peace? Scripture tells us to sing the praises of the Lord. Make a joyful noise.

Sometimes we get stuck on one note, a harsh vocalization of complaints. Instead of crying out to God in joy, we cry "Woe is me." Our joyful noise becomes only noise, much in the same way as Georgia May's song can become a complaint when it goes on too long.

Nowhere in the Bible are we told to "complain unto the Lord." We're told "Do all things without complaining" (Philemon 2:4). "Don't grumble against one another" (James 5:9).

God responded to the Israelites' moaning about not having enough food by giving them manna (Exodus 16:8). But what did they do? They got tired of it and complained some more (Numbers 11).

Before we get too cocky about not being as ungrateful as the Hebrews, we should ask ourselves if we're always happy what God has provided. We're often like the people Moses brought out of Egypt—grumbling and complaining.

Georgia May makes sounds at feeding time as though she hasn't been fed for days, even weeks. But when she gets the same old armful of hay, she settles in, and eats what she's given without a murmur.

I want to be like her. To sing when I'm happy, sing when I'm not, and all the while not complain.

> **Oh come, let us sing to the Lord; let us make a joyful noise to the rock of our salvation! Let us come into his presence with thanksgiving; let us make a joyful noise to him with songs of praise!**
> **—Psalm 95:1-2**

DONKEYS ARE SOCIAL

Most herd animals are social creatures. They like to be around others like themselves. I think, in addition to safety in numbers, there's security in being with the group.

Donkeys are no different, except in one way. They don't like to be alone and will socialize with most any creatures. One group of donkeys we had would graze in the same area where our dogs played. All were friends.

This part of their personality is what makes donkeys great guards for cattle herds. They like their cow friends so much, the donks will chase off predators.

Chucky, a donkey who lives on another ranch, is testament to what happens when left alone too long. He can appear to be mean and cranky.

Poor Chucky has lived in a small pasture by himself for more than ten years. When he got a chance to join a cattle herd, his actions betrayed his excitement. His encounters with the cows gave the appearance of being mean and attacking, but he was trying to be friendly. Before long, Chucky was sequestered to his little pasture again, and the cows were left in peace.

We humans aren't much different. We want—need—to be with others of our own kind. When we are kept away, or more accurately, keep ourselves away, we can get cranky.

We feel safe being with others like us. Plus, we like the added benefit of support.

I know. I know. Introverts are described as loners not wanting or needing other people. Not true. I know this because I'm an introvert. If I don't socialize occasionally, I become depressed. Mind you, a little of the herd goes a long way for me, but I still need them.

What happened to Elijah when he was alone in serving God? In his crusade against the Baals and the royalty, he was by himself. No one supported him. Elijah soon became so despondent, he ran away. Unable to carry on without others any longer, he lost his will to live. Elijah needed another donkey to be with him (1 Kings 19).

God tells us not to give up being with others like us. For most of us, that means spending our time with other Christians (Hebrews 10:24–25). We're even told we are to be in fellowship with God. Why? One reason may be to not become cranky donkeys.

Like our guard donkey pals, we encourage each other, teach each other, and yes, protect each other. We chase off the predator of souls when an attack is made against one of our herd.

God didn't intend for humans to be alone (Genesis 2:18). Our companionship with other people is a model for our companionship with God. Even if fallible humans fail us or leave us alone, God will not. Sometimes he'll send someone into our lives to be with us. Sometimes we need to get up and go to others. It doesn't matter. Find your herd and be with them.

That which we have seen and heard we proclaim also to you, so that you too may

have fellowship with us; and indeed our fellowship is with the Father and with his Son Jesus Christ.—1 John 1:3

NOW HE'S ALONE

When the three girls moved to another home, we still heard Jeb and Ellie May call for them from their home across the road. The calls were different. They were clearly asking, "Where are you?"

A few months later, Ellie May disappeared. We had no idea how she got out of the pasture, where she went, or why Jeb didn't follow. He was alone. The loneliness was heard in his calls.

Soon the cries for his friends decreased. Then they stopped. Oh, Jeb still joined the morning donkey grapevine. But he no longer hollered for his family. They were gone.

As time went on, more of the donkey neighbors moved. The morning chatter stopped. No more friendly bantering catching up on the pasture news.

After Jeb moved to our pasture, he was still lonely. While he was acclimating to his new home, we often went out to be sure he knew where the sweet feed was located, how to make his way to the hay feeder, and to be sure he couldn't work his way out of the gate. Still aloneness was evident. He only brayed to announce he was ready to eat.

Now, Neesy is his companion, and we hear more donkey talk during the day. I imagine they tease each other as siblings do, even though they aren't from the same biological family.

They've become family to each other. Jeb is no longer alone. He has a companion who sticks with him.

Sadly, many people are alone. They're left behind various reasons—friends and family move, a loved one dies, and in our overly fast world, no one has time to visit. Calls are made for a while, but eventually when no one answers, they stop.

Even when surrounded by people, we can feel abandoned and alone. We can even feel God has deserted us because we don't seem to hear him anymore.

Think of all those who've gone before us who had the same emotions. David wrote, "How long, O Lord? Will you forget me forever?" (Psalm 13:1). How much more alone could Jonah have felt in the belly of the giant fish? Jesus cried from the cross, "My God, my God, why have you forsaken me?" (Mark 15:34). Then came the morning, and God was there.

While we may be alone for a while, we are never deserted. Our companion, Jesus Christ, is walking with us, even when we don't see him.

It is the Lord who goes before you. He will be with you; he will not leave you or forsake you. Do not fear or be dismayed.
–Deuteronomy 31:8

IT'S A UNICORN

The rising sun gave only enough illumination in the field for me to make out the outline of the trees, fences, chicken coop, and the ... I saw a new outline.

The shape was familiar but not to our place. I easily recognized it as an equine of some type. The soft pre-dawn light showed this creature's pale color. Strange. And something appeared to extend from its forehead.

I woke my husband, who is more familiar with the area animals. "We either have a small white horse or a unicorn out there."

By the time Hubby had his pants and shoes on, the sun peeked over the horizon. In full daylight, I saw what animal had wandered up the driveway. A donkey.

Once we realized what sort of animal we had, we went out and learned the donkey was Jeb. He is a brother to one of the jennies we previously owned and lived across the road. Our neighbors wanted to find a new home for him. Jeb apparently found his own place to live.

A well-mannered therapy animal, Jeb originally came from a camp for special children. He followed me through the gate into the green fields. He moseyed off while Hubby called our neighbor to let him know of the morning's developments.

Jeb is now a part of the Peaceable Kingdom.

This isn't the only time I haven't seen things clearly. In fact, far too often in my life I look without the clarity of full light. I guess at what is ahead and move forward. Then the light shines, and I'm surprised I'm not seeing a unicorn.

Sometimes we move forward without God's light. We think we can see enough to know the way ahead. What we're actually seeing is a mere outline. We make decisions based on a partial view.

God wants the way ahead to be well lit. Sometimes he asks us to wait for him to fully illuminate the situation before we step forward.

When we allow God's light to shine, we'll have the full view of his best for us. Then we won't be chasing unicorns.

I am the light of the world. Whoever follows
me will not walk in darkness, but will have
the light of life. –John 8:12

SAMARITAN'S DONKEY

Did you know there's a donkey in the parable of the Good Samaritan (Luke 10:25–37)? Here's brief refresher: A man was beaten and left for dead along the side of the road. A priest and a Levite both passed by him. But a "despised" Samaritan (NLT) came by, helped the injured man, put him on his donkey, and took the fellow to an inn for further care.

Let's take a look at a character in the story few of us notice—a donkey. The Samaritan probably rode the donkey because camels were primarily used to carry loads of goods.

This donkey tells us a little about the Samaritan. In those days, donkeys were a sign of wealth, even royalty. So this Samaritan was probably wealthy and may have been a leader in his community.

In some cultures, the donkey symbolizes friendship and loyalty. I'm not surprised. Donkeys are social. Like other animals, and some people, will guard others and will help carry burdens.

More than representing the Samaritan's wealth and status, this donkey represented the despised person's friendship and loyalty to others without judgment. The Samaritan didn't judge the person along the road by appearance, but by need. He took that wounded man's burden and carried it. The beaten man was protected from further injury and possibly death because the Samaritan, like his donkey, was willing to serve without judgment or complaint.

Are we donkeys? Most of the time when we're accused of being a donkey, it refers to being stubborn. Let's take a moment and think about the other qualities of this beast of burden: friendship, loyalty, and trust.

- Do we help others, even when we're told it's a waste of time? Are we a friend of the friendless, the ones left alongside the road?
- Do we stick by others regardless of the circumstances? Do we protect people from the injury of gossip, loneliness, or injustice? Are we known to stick by another, no matter the situation?
- Do we humble ourselves like the meek donkey? Like the Samaritan? Are we willing to lift people up by carrying their burdens? Is *trustworthy* a word used to describe us?

I'm sad to say I don't always match these descriptions.

At the end of the parable, Jesus asked of the three people who were on the road that day, who was a neighbor to the beaten man. A listener responded, "The one who showed mercy."

To which Jesus said, "Yes. Now go and do the same."

I challenge you—I challenge myself—do the same as the Samaritan and his donkey. Be a loyal friend even to the stranger. Carry the burdens of others. Humble ourselves to protect the lowly.

You go, and do likewise.–Luke 10:37

DONKEY WHISPERER

A few people have called me a donkey whisperer. This rumor started when I was able to cajole Neesy up the road when pulling, pushing, and shouting didn't work. Something I learned early in my encounters with donkeys is they're gentle creatures that appreciate gentleness in return.

I decided to look to see if there's an official definition for an animal whisperer. There is. What the term means depends on who is being asked. Some call it a psychic ability to telepathically communicate with animals. Oh my goodness, if I could do that, I think I would use the gift with humans who don't agree with me.

On a different website, an "internationally acclaimed" animal whisperer lists a number of qualifications including diplomas and certificates. I have diplomas and certificates. None, however, are in programs involving animals.

Still another website—after all, the internet has become our source for facts—referred to an animal whisperer as an "inter-species communicator." Hmmm ... that's a catchy title: "Donkey Inter-Species Communicator."

Actually, the whole idea of being an animal whisperer is a source of family fun and laughter. My daughter asked if I could be both a donkey and chicken whisperer. The chickens come running when I call to them ... no whispering involved. They know if I'm calling them, they'll get fed. Not sure that communication counts for much.

Like most of God's creatures, donkeys will respond to a gentle hand. Time is needed to develop the communication. Not everyone has the personality to devote the amount of patience needed. Thus, they resort to harsher treatment.

Aren't we humans that way? Don't we respond to a gentle touch, a gentle word ... a whisper?

After Elijah defeated the Baals, he went to the mountains to meet with God (1 Kings 19:9–18). A fierce wind came, then an earthquake, followed by fire. God wasn't in any of these loud and fierce things. Verse 12 tells us "after the fire the sound of a low whisper." Sometimes this is referred to as the" still, small voice of God."

God does demonstrate his judgment with fierceness. But he woos us with gentleness. He came to us in the form of a man who lived a quiet life. Instead of the beatings we deserve, God whispers to us through Jesus.

I call to my donkeys. OK, I call to most any donkey. I can tell if one has been neglected or mistreated—it doesn't come near. I watch from afar. I'm not sure how an animal knows whether a person is going to be kind or mean; they seem to know.

I wait for the donkey to approach me. I reach out with a quiet voice, a palm–up hand, and slow movements. Several visits may be required, but eventually the animal will cautiously approach. Neesy behaved like that. My first encounter with her, I gave her water on a hot day. She knew I meant no harm. She followed me slowly up the road to her new home.

I'm not a donkey whisperer. I have no special ability. I talk gently and reach out to misunderstood animals. God calls us quietly and gently—he whispers. He reached out 2,000 years ago. We respond, sometimes with caution, to his whispers.

> **After the earthquake a fire, but the LORD was not in the fire. And after the fire the sound of a low whisper. And when Elijah heard it, he wrapped his face in his cloak and went out and stood at the entrance of the cave. And behold, there came a voice to him.—1 Kings 19:12–13**

WHAT MADE US THINK?

"Are you sure you're OK?" the vet asked as I lifted myself from the ground.

"Yeah," I said more boldly than I felt. Actually, I felt rather foolish.

"Are you sure?" he questioned again, reaching to help me.

I'm not sure what made Hubby and me think we could hold back a five-hundred-pound, spooked donkey. But we'd tried. And failed.

We'd recently adopted a female donkey and didn't want a herd of little donks, so Jeb needed a "procedure."

On the appointed day, we haltered Jeb and waited to greet Dr. Montgomery and his helper.

"Look." Dr. Montgomery's assistant, Don, walked up to corral. "This guy is ready to go. And he's so calm."

Don attached the lead to Jeb's halter and led him from the corral to a nearby shade tree. We stood by, thinking all would go well.

Mistake number one was letting our friendly lab mix see Dr. Montgomery. Jeb was already a bit unsettled being outside of his secure pasture. When ever-happy Molly bounced up to greet her friend, Jeb began to pace back and forth.

Once Molly was safely in the house, Dr. Montgomery and Don began preparing Jeb for the procedure. Don had a rope connected to Jeb's halter to hold him while Dr. Montgomery was ready with a shot of sedative to calm him before the anesthetic. Hubby and I each had an additional lead ... just in case. Well, "in case" happened.

When the vet attempted to give Jeb the first shot, he spooked and ran. *Oh, no.* That's when I realized mistake number two—the gate was still open. We had no other choice than to keep Jeb from bolting out the gate and down the road. Hubby and I dug in our heels and held on for a wild ride, while Don had wisely let go immediately.

Hubby went down first and Jeb dragged him a few feet in the gravel. Then I flew off my feet and landed on my sternum.

Jeb was free and galloping toward the open gate.

After checking our welfare, Dr. Montgomery jumped in his truck to retrieve the donkey. Upon his return, with Jeb trotting behind the truck, he tied the wayward donkey to a tree in a less desirable place for the operation.

While Jeb was out, and the vet was doing his deed, Hubby and I went in the house to clean up a little. We laughed at ourselves for thinking we could stop a terrorized donkey.

How many times do we hold on to something knowing full well it isn't going to end well? God clearly tells us we are to let go, but we don't. We insist we can continue holding on even when we know the outcome isn't going to be pretty.

The unexpected happens, and we continue to hold on. Life bolts, and we continue to hold on. We can believe circumstances become runaways, but still we continue to hold on.

What would have happened if we had let go of Jeb's lead at the first sign of trouble? He would've run out the gate.

But Hubby and I wouldn't have been injured. Our clinging to the rope didn't change the outcome.

Letting go doesn't always mean to give up doing what God has called you to do. Julia Attaway put it this way, "I've finally begun to understand that the phrase means something different. 'Let go [of the outcome you desire, and let God [manifest His will].'"[2]

The outcome with Jeb was the same: he ran out the gate into the road. We had a desired outcome of keeping him from running. We needed to let go of the donkey, and that outcome, to avoid falling on our faces. We didn't; we fell.

Trust me; we tried hard to prevent the inevitable. But in the end, Jeb's reaction won out. I'm not sure why we were worried about Jeb going into the road. We live near the end of a gravel road. It's not like he was charging into a four-lane freeway. In that moment, we had a plan.

God has a plan (Jeremiah 29:11). God knows better than we do what's ahead and how to avoid things ending in catastrophe. When we release our plans, no matter how detailed, we make room for God to do what he intended in the first place without injuring ourselves along the way.

God wants us to let go. He has the lead ... let him lead.

Trust in the Lord with all your heart, and do not lean on your own understanding. In all your ways acknowledge him, and he will make straight your paths.–Proverbs 3:5-6

THE DONKEY'S CROSS

When most of us think of a donkey, we visualize a gray or gray/brown animal with the familiar "lights" around the eyes, muzzle, and on the feet with a cross down the back that spreads across the shoulders. This donkey is commonly known as the Jerusalem donkey.

Legend tells us the little donkey, probably a foal, on which Jesus rode into Jerusalem on Palm Sunday knew he was going to be arrested and tortured. On the day of the crucifixion, the little donkey tried to get through the crowd to help Jesus carry the cross. But he couldn't.

After the spectacle died down and the crowd dispersed, the little donkey was so sad he turned his back on the cross where Jesus was hanging. In the waning light, the shadow of the cross landed on the donkey's back. Every donkey since has had a cross on its back. All donkeys have a cross. The marking doesn't show in the coat of the darker-colored donks but can be seen on their skin if the animal's hair is shaved.

Neesy is sorrel-colored, dark red. She has few of the common markings of donkeys. Her muzzle isn't white, she has no spots around her eyes, and no obvious cross on her back and shoulders. On closer inspection. Neesy's can be seen in the slightly darker hairs on her back and shoulders.

Science says the cross is the remnant of evolution. The theory is that donkeys are descendants of zebras and other wild equines that have stripes for camouflage. I like the legend better.

The donkey's variations in color and size reminds me God is creative. No creature is identical to another. They are unique. Neesy and Jeb are both uncommon colors, but they are donkeys just the same. And they carry the same cross markings.

The creative God has made each of us, even identical twins, unique in some way. But we all carry our own cross.

Our cross is not a legend of sorrow. Our cross is our sinful nature. Whether seen or not, we bear it. Jesus tells us to take up our cross and follow him.

As we confess the burden of sin we carry, the shadow of Christ's cross falls on us covering our sinful cross. When we take on his cross and follow him, our load becomes lighter, and the cross of Christ will be in full view for all to see.

Then Jesus told his disciples, "If anyone would come after me, let him deny himself and take up his cross and follow me."
–Matthew 16:24

JEB EATS BOXES

There he stood in his familiar place at the corner of the pasture by the driveway gate with a piece of cardboard hanging from his mouth. My first thought was *How did he get some cardboard?* When I looked more carefully and took in the whole scene, I saw cans of beans around his hooves. Sigh. I now saw the problem.

We had begun ordering a lot of our groceries online for home delivery. It's easier and cheaper than driving into town. On this particular day, we weren't home when the delivery truck arrived. Usually packages are dropped on the other side of the gate where they can't be seen from the road.

Apparently, a substitute driver placed the groceries right next to Jeb's nose. Goats are known for eating everything. Few realize donkeys are every bit as curious. Jeb pulled the box closer, ripped it opened, and shuffled through the canned goods. Apparently, he didn't want any beans, so he decided to snack on the box itself.

My plans for that hot July day were changed because I now had to retrieve my canned goods. Picking up groceries from between the hooves of a donkey wasn't on my schedule. All I could do while gathering the cans was chuckle. The delivery man didn't know he was setting a box near a mischievous donkey. Jeb was just being Jeb. It's hard to be angry with him or anyone.

I would have never set a box near *that* fence. But I knew a silly donkey lived there; the driver didn't. We still often laugh about this incident. My regret is not taking a picture of Jeb with the evidence in his mouth.

The other day we came home, and, again, found a package at that corner. Jeb was in a different pasture, so he didn't have an opportunity to rummage through this box. Considering it was full of canning jars, it might have been more dangerous to both donkey and human. I admonished myself for not making a sign to let delivery drivers know where to place the boxes when the gate is closed. But anger? No, I can't be angry. It would serve no purpose.

Sometimes we get angry because of inconvenience, or when someone does something seemingly illogical to us. But God tells us to be slow to anger (James 1:19). I could have been angry with Jeb or with the driver or even with myself. But there was no need. This has been difficult for me to master. Instead, I've learned to find humor when I can and be more tolerant of others. Anger serves no purpose and being slow to anger makes life more pleasant.

> **Know this, my beloved brothers: let every person be quick to hear, slow to speak, slow to anger; for the anger of man does not produce the righteousness of God.**
> **–James 1:19–20**

DONKEY CONTENTMENT

To carry a load without resting, to be not bothered by heat or cold, and to always be content: these things we can learn from a donkey.—Pakistani proverb

The temperature is a brutal 108. Yet Jeb stands in his usual resting position. In summer heat and winter cold, Jeb takes his afternoon rest near a scraggly oak tree next to the corral. That's where Jeb takes his afternoon rest.

Jeb, and for that matter the other donkeys we've had in our lives, doesn't seem to mind weather extremes. Well, they do hide from rain. I think the pounding water irritates their skin.

Have you ever noticed in stories about people trudging across deserts, they often have a donkey or two carrying the luggage—lots of luggage. Sturdier than horses, donkeys can carry a hefty load. They will also trudge along behind for hours and hours, only resting when their human companion needs a break.

My donkeys rarely complain. Oh, they do let us know, with a gentle reminder, when it's time to add feed to their buckets and bins. Look at a donkey's face. Yep, I encourage you to go find a donkey and look directly in the eyes. What will you see? Probably contentment.

How about us? Are we asked to carry a load, stand in the heat, or trudge through the cold? If so, will we do so without complaint? No, we complain whenever we get a chance. Whether to a loved one, God, or a stranger on an airplane, we seem to always have reason to voice our discontent.

How can we be more like our donkey friends? We can stand in the heat of trouble with God's peace. Strengthen ourselves to carry the burden of everyday life with the help offered through the Holy Spirit. While we may never know the secret of a donkey's contentment, we can learn contentment by rejoicing in the life God has graciously given to us.

I rejoiced greatly in the Lord ... For I have learned in whatever situation I am to be content.–Philippians 4:10-11

JEB AND THE FEED BUCKET

Donkeys are determined creatures. At least Jeb is. Once he's made up his mind to do something, especially when food is involved, he pushes forward with his plan. Yes, this donkey plans. His face shows the scheming.

Hurricane Harvey was on the radar, and we worried about Jeb being out in the wind and rain for several days. So, we battened down the hay, tightened the feed bucket lids, and added a gate from the corral to the little feed barn. When the storm approached, we opened the gate, and let Jeb shelter in the feed barn with Pumpkin, the donkey cat.

After Harvey blew over, we decided to make a stall with easier access to the corral. Jeb liked the stall. I often see him standing in it facing out watching the rain. Problem solved. Jeb is able to shelter out of inclement weather; the hay and feed were protected.

We had stashed other items in the barn—firewood, planks of wallboard, a few tools. Things no donkey would be interested in. Whether inside the barn or in his stall, Jeb didn't bother anything in the barn, not even the feed buckets.

Until one day when I went out to the corral to feed the pair. A piece of wall board had was lying in the corral. Hmmm. As I cleaned up the broken pieces of board, I figured one of the donkeys must have been bored and decided to play by dragging the board through the slats of the stall.

A couple weeks later, I found a flat plastic box with pieces of wood wedged under the hay crib. What? I'd heard equines will eat wood when hungry. These equines were anything but hungry. They have access to the pasture, so they'd have no reason to be bored. Then again, there's no reason for any kid to be bored either.

I pulled the box of wood back into the barn and looked around for any other temptations. I checked the hay crib to be sure it was firmly in place as well. Who knows what a determined donkey will do?

A few days later, I found a feed bucket laying on its side. I surmised some nocturnal animals had rummaged around, because I *knew* the donkeys couldn't reach them. Never underestimate a determined donkey.

One morning, I heard a strange thumping in the corral. I looked out and saw both donks near the feeding area. Neesy stood off to the side. Jeb was intent on something. I went to investigate, wondering if another creature had invaded their territory.

Nope. Another creature hadn't been involved. A donkey had invaded the feed barn. The bucket had been pulled out of the stall, and Jeb was making progress at getting it open. Hmm, how in the world did he do that?

Neesy nickered as if to say, "I had nothing to do with it. I tried to tell him not to."

I grabbed the bucket, admonishing Jeb for his misdeed. I still wondered how he got that bucket. He watched my every step without remorse. He was planning his mischief.

When I rounded the corner into the barn and could see the end of the stall, I saw the hay crib was out of place. But the gap between the ground and the metal bar holding the feeder out of the dirt wasn't big enough for either donkeys' shoulders to push through. So, still I wondered *How did that bucket roll out of the barn, through the stall, and into the corral?*

I set the bucket back in its place, readjusted the lid, moved the crib to the center of the bar, and turned to leave. Before I was out of the barn, I heard the grating of the crib against the metal bar.

I spun around and almost couldn't believe what I saw. Jeb was hunkered down, stretching his neck through the opening to reach that feed bucket.

Moving the crib apparently had become an easy task for this five-hundred-pound beast. Yes, at the moment, my loving jack donkey was a beast. Don't underestimate the determination of a donkey.

I chased both donks out of the corral and rearranged the feed buckets and other supplies in the barn far away from the rubber-necked equine.

Jeb continues to try and get at those feed storage buckets. He now knows his sweet feed is in them. He keeps trying to get to them. He even reached in and tried pulling the pallet they sit on toward the stall. We've anchored it in place.

Jeb wasn't hungry. In addition to twice-daily feedings, he has plenty of grass to graze on. What started as a bored animal's game turned into a quest.

I get bored sometimes too. I'll admit there are times I get bored with my Christian life. Read the Bible, pray (or rather repeat words), worship ... again ... ho, hum. Instead of turning to the lush fields God has for me, I decide I need to do something different.

Don't think I wander off to other religions. Unlike Jeb, who finds something else to do, I quit doing what I need to. God has to shake things up and put me in a new place where I can find refreshment and excitement in him again.

Once the shaking has stopped, I wonder why I became so bored. Why did I wander off from what I knew was a good thing? Why did I get myself into trouble? Because I'm human.

God never leaves us. He doesn't turn his back and walk away. He doesn't get bored with caring for us. Like a loving shepherd, he guides us back to the joy and peace found in his lush pastures.

For you were straying like sheep, but have now returned to the Shepherd and Overseer of your souls.–1 Peter 2:25

A THRASHER

Travels with a Donkey in Cevennes is Robert Louis Stevenson's log of his travels through France with a donkey as his companion. The author describes the jenny he named Modestine as no larger than a St. Bernard and diminutive. When he prepared to purchase her, the previous owner talked about her gentle nature.

Being a novice to hiking as well as to handling donkeys, Stevenson began using a kind touch with Modestine. Not long into his journey, though, a man came along who thrashed poor Modestine into running. Stevenson concluded this was an effective way to move the lowly creature faster along the route and in areas a donkey might balk.

Of course, I had to remember as I read of this treatment, animals weren't given the same care and considerations in the late 1800s as they are today. Stevenson did call the treatment effective if inhumane and never did seem comfortable with the harsh treatment.

Not all animals respond to thrashing as Modestine did. Some become mean and may attack their owner. But I've come to the conclusion most donkeys react to thrashing as calmly as they do to a whisper.

Donkeys will respond to a gentle hand ... and a few treats. Some people, like Stevenson, may not know another way to train an animal. And not everyone has the personality to devote the patience needed. Thus, they resort to tougher treatment.

Aren't we humans that way too? Don't we respond better to a tender touch, a gentle word ... a whisper? How often, though, do we lash out at others with a tongue thrashing? I confess, sometimes I finish a verbal onslaught and am horrified at what I did.

Jesus gave us examples of responding with a gentle, quiet word—a healing word. His whisper changed lives, drew people to him and to God. When the religious leaders brought an adulterous woman to him for rebuke. (John 8:1–11) Jesus didn't say much to anyone. He quietly said, "Let him who is without sin among you be the first to throw a stone at her" (v. 7). To the woman, he said, "Go, and from now on sin no more" (v. 11).

No wrath. No thrashing. Only quiet words that taught lessons and healed souls.

The wise writer of Proverbs tells us that a gentle tongue is life. The word *gentle* can be translated "healing." Whether to a donkey or another person, kindness teaches—gentleness heals. Oh, that I might speak as tenderly to others as I do to Jeb and Neesy.

A gentle tongue is a tree of life, but
perverseness in it breaks the spirit.
–Proverbs 15.4

MR. NOT-SO-DONKEY-FRIENDLY

"We need some help," Hubby's text message said, followed with "and bring some water."

Earlier, I'd offered to assist in moving Neesy the mile from her former home to our little ranch. Because it was only a mile, they decided walking her would be the best choice. Hubby was sure the trip wouldn't take long. But the task turned into a greater undertaking than anticipated.

Neesy is an Eeyore-type of a donkey. She seemed sad and lonely most of the time, even though she had been with a couple horses. Horses can be stuck-up creatures, you know. But when her companions died, she needed new friends. We also knew Jeb needed more than Pumpkin the cat as a friend.

The moving day grew hot and muggy with thunderstorms threatening. One of the helpers was an impatient man and made it known he didn't like Neesy anyway. So, I braced myself for a disaster.

Few donkeys have shoes. They're only needed for those who will be on hard surfaces, like streets. Most of the donkeys in our area live in pastures. I'm not sure why someone made the decision to walk her down the middle of the road, which can be as hard as asphalt. Poor Neesy's feet began to hurt.

At one point, Mr. Not-So-Donkey-Friendly thought a good plan was to tie her to the back of a truck and drag her.

He was sure she'd start walking. As she was dragged along the gravel, her already sore hooves became injured.

That's when Hubby sent me the text message.

They had made it about halfway when I arrived. I took the water right to Neesy. Those humans could go find their own. I hadn't thought to grab the bag of treats, so Hubby went back for some.

Mr. Not-So-Donkey-Friendly had a few not-so-nice things to say.

Neesy strained to get off the gravel and onto the soft shoulder of the road.

Mr. Not-So-Donkey-Friendly said, "No, you don't get to have the grass until you get to your new home."

Incensed with his dreadful attitude, I untied her lead from the truck and moved her to the side of the road. Those standing and watching my actions were surprised when she started walking behind me. We walked a few steps, she stopped to nibble. I talked gently to her as we moved on.

I'm sure Mr. Not-So-Donkey-Friendly didn't understand and may have wondered *Why is that stupid donkey so stubborn with me?*

Donkeys aren't stubborn. They're cautious. When someone unfriendly comes near, they tend to stop and not budge out of fear of what might happen.

How often do we simply follow because those around us are moving in a particular direction? How often do we walk a gravel road, which hurts, but we keep going in spite of the pain? The pain is meant to be a warning. Sometimes we humans need to be a little more stubborn ... er ... cautious.

God tells us to choose our companions wisely, not to be followers, except of him. He is the gentle shepherd. He knows we need the green grasses, especially when the way is hot and scary. He leads us to the lush pastures (Psalm 23).

When we come to a fork in the road, we need to, as Robert Frost described in the poem *The Road Not Taken*, be thoughtful about which one to take: the well-traveled gravel road or the less-traveled grassy road. Be stubborn as the donkey and refuse to walk the painful well-trodden path. Follow God on the greener way.

And they will say to you, "Look, there!" or "Look, here!" Do not go out or follow them.–Luke 17:23

DELIGHT

Donkeys don't run with the sleek grace of a horse. A donkey forges forward with head down and legs churning. I've watched my two chase each other around the pasture as though they're in training, not quite knowing which foot to put in front of the other.

Each morning, Jeb and Neesy get a scoopful of sweet feed, a mixture of grains lathered with molasses. After filling their food bins, I head to the feed barn to gather food for the other animals and to fill the hay cribs for the donks.

It's not unusual to hear donkey fussing, a noise not quite the same as the hew-haw sound they usually make. Jeb pushes his way past Neesy to run down the corral toward the barn. His head is up; he's focused on his destination. It's not the hay. It's a handful of corn.

Corn isn't part of their usual feeding routine. It is a treat. To say Jeb delights in it might be an understatement.

Watching him run in his lumbering manner down the corral toward me brings a smile to my face. It's comical to watch. And seeing him head toward me in anticipation of the treat is joyful. Jeb delights in his handful of corn.

One morning as I opened the bucket of corn, I looked up. Seeing Jeb's joy in waiting for the treat, I wondered, *Do I run to God with the same anticipation of delight?*

Psalm 37:4 says "Delight yourself in the Lord, and he will give you the desires of your heart." It's our human tendency to focus on what we can get rather than what we are giving. We will get what we want if we are happy with God. In fact, God says, "For the Lord will again take delight in prospering you, as he took delight in your fathers" (Deuteronomy. 30:9). God will be happy when he gives us what we want. I'm good with that.

In a quick search of the book of Psalms, I found more than two dozen passages about delighting in God's law or commands—his instructions for us. Ten in Psalm 119 alone.

It's easy to be happy with God when it involves me getting what I want—my desires. What about delighting in what God wants? Am I as happy with his desires? I get excited as I sing praises to God, anticipating the desires of my heart. Do I take joy in God's commands, which are designed to bless me? Make me happy? I'm afraid not.

Gladly obeying my Lord shouldn't be a struggle. He blessed me abundantly above all I can imagine. My delight should be as Jeb's running for a handful of corn. I don't go to Jeb with the corn; he comes to me. Still, he's delighted.

As we approach God humbly in obedience, seeking what he has for us, joy and happiness is ours.

Jeb's joyful run to retrieve a mere handful of corn looks funny. I'm reminded I need to joyfully run to God in obedience, no matter how awkward it may seem.

Lead me in the path of your commandments, for I delight in it.—Psalm 119:35

NESTOR

In the sea of children's Christmas shows with the likes of Rudolph, Frosty, and the Grinch, the tale of *Nestor, The Long-Eared Christmas Donkey* never seems to make it to the list of Christmas movies for children.

The story is simple. Nestor is different; he has unusually long ears—even for a donkey. As an oddling, Nestor was teased and ultimately rejected. Even his owner threw him out of the stable, leaving him to die in a snowstorm. Ultimately, through a series of miraculous events, Nester becomes the donkey Mary rides to Bethlehem.

The Bible is full of misfits; those who don't quite belong. David, the boy too small for Saul's army. Rahab was a prostitute. Deborah, a female judge. Zacchaeus, a short tax collector. Each of these oddballs has a purpose in God's plan. God used each in a unique way.

Does their uniqueness make them better suited for God's work? I'm not sure. I think God uses the misfits—those who don't quite fit in—because they don't fit in. Because they are rejected by current culture.

Here's the thing: Each of us relates to being a misfit. I doubt many of us are thinking, "That's not me. I'm not the odd one out." We can relate to the long-eared donkey and to being rejected. We think we aren't of much value to God's kingdom. We think we're Nestor.

David became king. Rahab was an ancestor of Jesus. Deborah led an army (unheard of in her culture). Zacchaeus, a reviled sinner, hosted a party for Jesus. Let's face it. Jesus's birth was surrounded by rumor and tales of infidelity. Conceived out of wedlock, he too may have been considered a misfit. Ultimately, he was rejected by nearly all.

God uses the misfits, the ugly ducklings, the long-eared donkeys to further his kingdom. Why? God doesn't care about our standing in society, the balance (or lack thereof) of our bank account, or the brand name of our clothes. For that matter, God doesn't even care about our long ears. God cares about us. He has a purpose for us. Maybe not to carry the mother of the Savior but to serve him.

> **For the Lord sees not as man sees: man looks on the outward appearance, but the Lord looks on the heart.–1 Samuel 16:7**

WHAT'S IN A NAME?

The term *ass* is rarely used in polite company these days. But in earlier times, even some translations of the Bible, this word was used in the place of the word *donkey*.

Merriam-Webster Collegiate Dictionary tells us an ass is "any of several hardy gregarious African or Asian perissodactyl mammals smaller than the horse and having long ears." Yep, that pretty well covers a donkey.

Some of the synonyms listed are burro, donkey, jackass (which is actually a specific breed), and moke (British slang). I like moke. But I'm not sure others would understand me when I talk about my mokes. Then there's the scientific name for a donkey, *Equus asinus*, which roughly translates to ass.

The first known use of the word *donkey* is about 1785. No one is sure exactly where the term came from, but there are several theories. One prevailing thought is the term originated from "dun," which is the dull, grey-brown. The shorten version, "donk" came into use mid-nineteenth century.

In our culture, we tend to name our animal friends. Why? Because names are important to us. Over the decades, the word *ass* has become a derogatory term and is rarely used when referring to our friendly donkeys. The name has changed.

God changed people's names to signify a change in that person's life—a new vision or new mission for that person. Abram and Sarai became Abraham and Sarah—when God made a covenant with Abram. Jacob became Israel when he engaged directly with God. Jesus chose Simon to carry on the message when he was gone, changing his name to Peter—the rock.

One name hasn't changed since creation—God. His unchanging name is an indication of God's unchanging nature. He is the "same yesterday and today and forever" (Hebrews 13:8). We know him because he is eternally the same. We depend on him because he doesn't change.

For I the LORD do not change.—Malachi 3:6

ANOTHER SIDE OF THE STORY

Sometimes as I look at Jeb and Neesy, I think I know what they'd say if they were to speak to me. Most often their talk would have something to do with food. I enjoy my imaginary tales of woe. I'm sure they wish I'd listen to them more attentively because they may have more to say.

Of course, Hubby thinks the same thing. If I'd only listen to what he's saying. Hubby is a retired electrician and still tinkers in the field. When he starts talking "electric" to me, I'm as clueless as I am with donkey-speak. My brain goes into the overload, and the hearing portion stops working. I don't get the full impact of what he's telling me. My brain stops somewhere between amps and watts, and I only hear a portion of what he says.

We can easily get stuck on one part of a story. For a multitude of reasons, we stop listening or only hear the parts we think we understand. Too often, this is how gossip begins. Someone relates information they've received— well, part of the information. Often the juiciest piece of the story, the negative part. Or we may stop listening before the end of the story.

One morning my devotional reading included the story of Balaam, a story I've read often. After all, his encounters with God through a small donkey is part my love affair with these animals. This time, though, I decided not to stop at the end of the Numbers 22 where Balaam's conversation with his donkey occurs. I went on and learned there's more to Balaam's story—more to God's story.

Most of our lessons about the talking donkey end at verse 35. "And the angel of the Lord said to Balaam, 'Go with the men, but speak only the word that I tell you.' Balaam went with the princes of Balak" (Numbers 23:5)

Did Balaam obey God? Was the trip to see Balak the only purpose? What in the world happened next?

Balaam does go to Moab as God instructed. At the end of chapter 22, we're told, "And in the morning Balak took Balaam and brought him up to Bamoth-baal, and from there he saw a fraction of the people" (v. 41).

By not going any further, we don't get the fullness of the message.

When we continue, we learn Balaam partially listened to God. Balaam told Balak he would find out what God had to say then report back. God again repeated the nation of Israel was to be blessed, not cursed. Rather than curse the Hebrews as Balak requested, Balaam blessed. Three times the two men went through the same exercise: Balaam inquires of God. God says bless, not curse. Balak is unhappy.

Was Balaam a godly prophet seeking to serve God? No. He did what he thought would give him profit and acclaim. We're not here to judge Balaam's actions. The point of this story is not Balaam's obedience, or lack thereof. It's to grasp that we need to listen or read all the details before deciding about someone or a situation. We truly need "the rest of the story."

And as you wish that others would do to you, do so to them.–Luke 6:31

NEESY NEEDS LOVE

Neesy wasn't a happy donkey the hot day she moved to our ranchette. The one-mile trek had been made worse by walking on the gravel road.

When we finally walked her through the gate, rain started, and we decided to leave her standing by the gate. Honestly, I was wet and tired and didn't want to prod, poke, and push her to the pasture. So Neesy was left looking like Eeyore.

The next morning, she had made her way up to the green grass near the house. With treats in hand, I went out to greet our new family member. I was a bit taken back when Neesy had a greeting for me.

Without hesitation, Neesy walked over and started to rub her head on my belly. I'd never had a belly rub quite like that. I wrapped my arm around her neck while she expressed her love.

We've learned this is Neesy's way of greeting everyone. She'll even forego treats to have a moment to express her love to people. Our granddaughter laughed at Neesy's greeting the first time they met. Neesy doesn't only want to express her love; she also needs love.

Although she wasn't an abused donkey, Neesy didn't have much interaction with people. The horse she'd been corralled with had died, and she'd been alone for some time. Neesy wants love and is willing to share it with others.

We all need love. Some of us have a harder time sharing it as openly as Neesy. We want to give love, but it doesn't come out as demonstrative.

God knows our love need, and he provides it. The Scripture tells us hundreds of times of God's love for us. It is described as:

- Steadfast love (Psalm 106:1)
- Huge in loyal love (Numbers 14:18 MSG)
- Abounding in love (Nehemiah 9:17)
- Relentlessly loves (1 Kings 8:23 MSG)
- His love never quits (Jeremiah 3:13)
- Unfailing love (Psalm 36:5 NLT)
- Tons of love (Nehemiah 9:16–19 MSG)
- Extravagant love (1 John 3:1 VOICE)

He has shown no greater love than to send his son to die for our sins (John 3:16). Oh, how he loves us. We should be Neesys and take joy in sharing love with others. After all, God has shown love to us.

For God so loved the world, that he gave his only Son, that whoever believes in him should not perish but have eternal life.
–John 3:16

PUMPKIN'S TRUST

Our cat Pumpkin was raised in a donkey shed near their pasture. I'm not sure if he thinks they're gigantic felines, or if he's a miniature version of them. He has no fear being around the five-hundred-pound creatures.

We've watched in amazement as Pumpkin walks between their legs. On an occasion or two, I've seen Jeb and Pumpkin nose to nose as though exchanging greetings. Neesy isn't quite as familiar with this little creature sauntering around her while she eats. But she doesn't balk at the cat or attempt to shoo Pumpkin away.

One morning, I headed back to the feed barn to fill the bird feeder, I saw Pumpkin and Jeb once again sharing time together. Pumpkin was lying beneath the hay feeder with scraps of hay on his back, and Jeb was grabbing mouthfuls of the hay he spilled on the ground. Neither animal seemed bothered by the other. Jeb ate, Pumpkin relaxed after his breakfast.

What trust!

I grabbed my phone to take a picture. I knew no one would believe me if I tried to explain this relationship. These two are truly the odd couple.

Pumpkin was born and spent the first year of his life in adverse conditions. A couple of months before he moved to the Peaceable Kingdom, he was mauled by a large dog.

He still bears the scar on his neck. Pumpkin's home was a small shed the donkeys used for shelter in rain. He had every reason to be fearful. Instead, Pumpkin learned trust.

Pumpkin teaches me there's more to trust than not expecting bad to happen. It is placing confidence in the relationship. As Pumpkin lies with hay on his back, he trusts Jeb won't harm him. This cat is confident in his relationship with his donkey friend.

Am I that trusting? I admit I've become cynical with so much evil in our world. I don't trust other people readily and find myself wondering about their motives. I confess, at moments these thoughts spill over to my relationship with God. *God, do I trust you as much as Pumpkin trusts the donkeys?* Oh, I hope so. I pray so. *Father God, teach me to have the same calm trust in you.*

The fear of man lays a snare, but whoever trusts in the Lord is safe.—Proverbs 29:25

MOVING DONKEYS

Because cattle ranches surround the Peaceable Kingdom, we often see animals moved. Cattle and horses need to be moved to allow grasses to grow and to be sure other fields don't get overgrown. Smaller ranches will simply walk the animals to the desired location. Some larger ranches have cowboys. Yes, people sitting atop a horse, guiding the animals where they need to go. And sometimes gathering up the wayward ones that strike out on their own.

One would think trotting our donkeys down the driveway to the other pasture is simple by comparison. Sometimes we stroll causally from one area to the other. Sometimes it's more harrowing.

Our eleven-year-old granddaughter helped one summer. This city girl enjoys the tasks around our tiny ranch. Whether fetching eggs each day, hauling hay to the feeders, or moving animals, she jumps right in with few reservations.

Lynn has been around donkeys since she was barely the height of their bellies. Like Pumpkin, she trusts them. Now that she's taller than their backs, we let her graduate to a new task. Some may feel a wisp of a girl barely fifty pounds can't handle a five-hundred-pound beast. When Lynn is in charge, the donkey stroll is smooth. All creatures get moved. And a little girl has had a delightful day.

Sometimes we move the donkeys one at a time. Sometimes we move them separately. When our son visited, we decided to move the donkeys and do it as a group. Each adult could handle one donkey. Three donkeys, three adults—the math worked.

When moving the "herd" as a group, we generally move single file to avoid the animals weaving back and forth amongst each other, tangling leads and people. Hubby was in front, son Jack second in line, and I brought up the end of the parade. Just when we thought all was going well, it wasn't.

For reasons I'll never understand, Hope shoved Jack into the yucca tree. If you're not familiar with yucca trees, their long leaves have vicious spikes at the end. Being pricked by one is painful, being shoved into a dozen or so can be like falling into a spike trap.

Being a tough guy, Jack pushed back on the donkey, and continued the trek to the other pasture. Jack wasn't without injury. But he was more determined than the donkey to get the job done. He wasn't going to let this mere animal push him around.

We get like that with God sometimes. We decide we have a better plan, and we push and shove against the good God has for us. But unlike a donkey causing injury to the human, God isn't injured by our rebellion—we are.

How amazingly patient God is with us. He lets us go. Sometimes we end up in a mess of yucca leaves. But he's always there waiting for us to turn around and return to the path he laid out. God picks up the lead rope and take us to the pasture where we have time to feed on the nourishment he provides.

Trying to understand why we veer from God's path is as difficult as trying to understand why Hope pushed Jack into the yucca. It's not the why that matters so much. It's the fact we do go our own way. More importantly though, God is always ready to continue the journey with us on the road he has laid.

Many are the plans in the mind of a man,
but it is the purpose of the Lord that will
stand.–Proverbs 19:21

NEESY FOLLOWS JEB

It took a few days for Jeb to accept Neesy into his pasture. He'd been alone for several years, and this space was his. As is the way of donkeys, he did want some company. But he wanted his company to stay on the other side of the fence. A visit now and then was fine ... nothing full time.

After a few hours of typical donkey amorous behavior, Jeb and Neesy settled into a pushing and shoving relationship. Mostly Jeb pushing Neesy away from the hay rack and the feed buckets. Setting up separate, but nearby, areas solved the problem.

At this point in their less-than-loving relationship, they stay away from one another. However, they also stay within sight of each other. I never saw them completely hidden from each other. Thus, life went on in their corner of the Peaceable Kingdom, even if less than peaceable in the donkey pasture.

A few months went by before I noticed a change in behavior. As they moved around the corral and pasture, Neesy followed Jeb. If he moved into the trees, she did also. If he came to the water tank, she wasn't far behind. I don't think this was female subservient behavior. I think previously Neesy was being cautious.

She was in a new pasture. Neesy didn't know the territory. She didn't know what dangers might lurk. Jeb had lived here for a couple years. He knew the paths of the previous donkeys and had created some of his own. He knew the other animals that roamed through.

Neesy wasn't sure. But she could follow Jeb and know she would be safe. She put her trust in his donkey wisdom.

Who do we follow? Are we cautious about what might be lurking in the unseen areas?

Sadly, sometimes we follow the loudest or best-looking without caution. We allow ourselves to be led to the dark forest where sin is lurking. We don't have the cautious nature of our donkey friends. We push forward into the unknown.

Neesy spent time watching Jeb. Learning his behavior. Making sure he was trustworthy. After all, in the beginning of their relationship he was just another male donkey.

We too need to take time to watch someone's behavior, listen to their words, see who they gather around themselves. We need to exhibit the same donkey caution, even if it means not moving forward. Even if the person is a leader in the Christian community, be sure they're someone God wants *you* to follow.

God will reveal his leaders. He'll show us who we are to follow—the one who knows the safe path through the unknown territories.

Before we can know who God wants us to follow, we have to know God. He is the ultimate leader; he knows the paths ahead. He has made a way for us if we will observe and take care of who we go after.

My sheep hear my voice, and I know them, and they follow me.—John 10:27

A GOD THING

One of my favorite phrases is "It's a God thing." I've often looked back to see how God has orchestrated events in my life. No other way is possible to explain them. The arrival of Jeb was one of those God things.

Spring came to Central Texas, and the grasses were growing tall one year because of abundant rain. Our grassy pastures aren't easy to mow because we haven't cleared trees away. Previously, our donkeys served as a grass-clearing crew. Now, we had no animals in the fields, so no mowing was being done.

We talked and prayed about whether to get donkeys again or get a few goats to clear the grass. The morning the "unicorn" showed up, we knew God answered our prayers. We would get donkeys.

God's provision didn't end. During the prior year, we had also begun raising chickens. We were feeling as though we understood the process well enough to increase our flock. I thought the best way was to get a rooster and let the hens hatch and raise the chicks. Hubby wasn't so sure. Once again, we prayed.

Jeb had been settled into his new digs for about two weeks when I glanced out the window—a rooster. A beautiful white rooster stood in the driveway. Hubby went out, opened the gate, and Goofy, the name we eventually gave him, marched right in. Goofy joined the flock as though he was meant to be there. I think he was.

The saying goes, "Hindsight is twenty-twenty." Hindsight also allows the opportunity to look back to realize what God has done for us. Sometimes, only in this looking back can we see God's hand in our affairs.

We can then have the assurance God will provide for us in the future. Nothing is beyond his control. Especially during times when we don't understand what's going on, looking for the God thing helps us to see our way through.

God does supply our needs, even when we don't know we have the need.

My God will supply every need of yours according to his riches in glory in Christ Jesus.–Philippians 4:19

NO LIGHT POINTS

Very few people know or care about donkey genetics. I don't know much and can't say I care all that much. But I've learned a couple things over the years with my long-eared friends.

Donkeys have "light points." These are areas of white or cream-colored hair around the muzzle, eyes, and belly. When I read about light points, I realized Neesy has none. I even looked closely at her pictures to be sure. Hmmmm.

In the donkey world, this is a genetic mutation, which can occur in all breeds of donkeys. Neesy is special.

Sometimes a mutation is thought of as a mistake. I remind my children and grandchildren God makes no mistakes. The same is true with mutations. They aren't mistakes; they make the creature special.

Donkeys are usually pictured as the dun- or grayish-colored animals. Both Neesy and Jeb are unusual. Jeb is a spotted donkey. Neesy is a dark sorrel (red), which is a combination of black and dun genes. (Bet you never wanted to know so much about donkey genetics.)

More people are more attracted to Jeb, our spotted donkey, than to our special Neesy. Spotted donkeys are rarer than the solid colored and are unique to the United States. Even though Neesy is also a lesser-known color, she's only seen as a smaller, dark-haired donkey ... nothing special. They don't see how special she is.

Each one of God's creatures are handmade, individual, unique. Even you and me. Did you know he counts each one of our hairs? I'm willing to bet no two people have the same number of strands just as no two people have the same fingerprints. We are handcrafted and distinctive.

God could have easily made each of us the same, like holiday cookies. I think there's a reason. We are each designed for a unique purpose. What would be the special purpose of a donkey with an unusual color and mutation? Maybe Neesy's sole purpose is to show the creativity of God. Just like Neesy, we are each special.

I praise you, for I am fearfully and wonderfully made.–Psalm 139:4

SOCIAL CREATURES

Jeb nipped. Neesy pushed back. Jeb blocked the stall. Neesy whined like a baby. Typical behavior of siblings, right? These two aren't siblings. Just a couple of donkeys who share the same space.

Each has their own feeder because they can't seem to stand at one feeder side-by-side and eat. Like children, they need to be separated. Later in the day, though, these two bickering donkeys are grazing together contentedly near each other.

When moving them from one pasture to another, we've learned it's best to walk Jeb over first. If he's left behind, not only does he holler and fuss, but Neesy constantly stops to graze as though waiting for her friend to join her.

On a recent trek across the property, Neesy thought Jeb had been gone too long without her. She hollered softly—a donkey always hollers, but there are occasions it's not quite as loud. Jeb immediately stopped eating the lush, new grass, perked his ears, and called back to her.

When we haltered Neesy and started the trek, she nearly ran. If allowed to have her way, she would have run. It's possibly she would have broken through a fence to get near him.

The next morning when the time came to give them their treat of sweet feed, the pushing and nipping started again.

But they were side-by-side as they wanted to be. Just like a couple children.

Donkeys are social animals. They aren't happy alone. Peaceful Valley Donkey Rescue, the largest donkey rescue in the country, requires adoption applicants to have either other equines on the property or agree to adopt at least two donkeys "to provide companionship."

We humans are social animals as well. As Christians, we are told to gather together not only for worship but also for meals and fellowship. Jesus enjoyed social gatherings.

But don't we all too often nip at our friends? Block the stall? Yes. I'm not sure why, but it seems more so in our Christian communities. Soon, either we or another member of the community leave, and we sadly sit alone looking for companionship wherever we can find it.

Before Neesy came to live with us, Jeb lingered at the fence dividing his pasture from the neighbor's. He waited for his horse pals to come for a meal. It always looked like an equine coffee klatch in the mornings. He was lonely. When a human came near the corral, he ran, such as a donkey runs, to talk.

Don't we do the same thing? We find our tribe and gather.

It's not a bad thing to be alone sometimes. It's comforting to sit with a loved one or a beloved friend and say nothing, quietly side-by-side. Jeb is much happier with a donkey pal than with the horse buddies. He rarely waits by the fence anymore.

Are you waiting by the fence? Or are you standing alone in a pasture? Go find your people. Don't get bogged down with the bickering, nipping, and stall blocking. It won't be long before you'll be side-by-side with companions, grazing contentedly.

And let us consider how to stir up one
another to love and good works, not
neglecting to meet together as is the habit
of some, but encouraging one another.–
Hebrews 10:24-25

DONKEYS: RIDE OF KINGS

If you've had the opportunity to spend much time around donkeys, you know they don't normally run a lot. Occasionally, I've seen our donkeys run around the pasture briefly. And I mean for only a little spurt. Sometimes Jeb will run to the hay feeder. That's only so he can get to the meal before his companion.

For the most part, donkeys mosey. Usually head down at a steady but slow pace. Not in a hurry and not harried. Few of us will watch a donkey and think, "Hmmm ... that's a ride fit for a king." In fact, though, donkeys *are* the ride of the kings.

Beginning in Genesis when Jacob blesses his sons, he declares Judah the ruling line—the family out of which the kings of Israel will come. As part of that blessing, a donkey represents his ride (Genesis 49:11).

Jair, a judge of Israel for twenty-two years, gave his sons donkeys to ride to the thirty towns they were to govern (Judges 10). And later we see Abdon, another judge of Israel, give his sons and grandsons donkeys as symbols of their authority.

Why a donkey instead of a horse? A horse is a symbol of power. The donkey not so much.

Because of their quiet, humble appearance, a donkey has over the ages become a symbol of peace. Solomon rode a donkey into Jerusalem to establish his kingship, a peaceful kingship, after he took the throne. Not just any donkey, King David's donkey (1 Kings 33).

The donkeys were a sign of a peaceful king coming. A ruler, not a warrior.

Ever watch a battle scene in a historical movie. No army goes in on donkeys. The larger, faster horses do the battle. The donkey is the peacekeeper. In fact, the Bible mentions donkeys being given to the victorious soldiers after a battle (Numbers 31).

We want to be known as people of peace. Too often we charge in as though riding to battle on a horse. How many arguments would cease if one of the parties would lead as a king on a donkey? Nope, we charge in on our horses—usually our high horse.

Let's learn to mosey through life, head down, watching the path. Not looking around for the next thing to win over. We can be royalty by being donkeys.

**Behold, your king is coming to you
righteous and having salvation is he,
humble and mounted on a donkey, on a colt,
the foal of a donkey.–Zechariah 9:9**

AS BORED AS A DONKEY

It happened again. We returned home to find Jeb and Neesy at the fence corner by the entrance gate, happily chewing a cardboard box. I failed to put up the warning sign, and the delivery man dropped the package within range of the curious donkeys.

These two seem to like the box best. Other items wrapped in plastic were set aside, or rather kicked aside, so they could get to anything encased in cardboard. By the time we returned home that day, the delivery box was nearly devoured, and they were working on the boxes other items arrived in.

Why are donkeys interested in a cardboard box set by the gatepost? We often question why our donkeys do the things they do.

When we had our three jennies, I noticed they were chewing through the trunk of a downed tree. Concerned about possible side effects, I asked our vet. He said donkeys get bored. Like a six-year-old child, when bored and left on their own, they find something to do. On the particular day mentioned above, their chosen activity was to devour a cardboard box.

Donkeys can be determined as well. Getting the box close enough to start the demolition wasn't easy for them. One of them, probably Jeb, the master at attaining forbidden items, reached through the barbed wire fence. Whether he pawed it until he broke a side or reached through and grabbed it with his teeth, we'll never know. Once the destruction began, he and Neesy had a good time.

Don't we get bored? A shiny, new thing comes along, or even a dull cardboard box full of the mundane, and we grab hold. We set aside that which doesn't seem to be tasty enough or shiny enough.

Have you ever been bored at a worship service? We think things like *we sang that song last month*, or *the pastor says the same prayer every week*. When we're supposed to be standing before Almighty God and giving him glory, we are slouched in muck of our own making.

Think about who we worship—the Creator of the universe, the all-powerful, the One. How in the world could our lives with him get boring? What has happened to the early excitement of worshipping our Lord? What changed? Truly, not God.

1. Worship time becomes too familiar. We get into ruts. Oh, we put nice names on them, like routine. But it's actually a rut. One writer wrote about his rut of reading the Bible daily. Reading God's Word each day isn't a bad thing. In fact, isn't that what we're taught when we first start our walk with Christ? After several years, though, it becomes a chore rather than a joy. This man found the awe of Jesus walking on water gone. He was too familiar. He decided he needed to break the cycle of read, pray, repeat. He didn't read the Scripture for several weeks and went back to it with renewed vision.

2. We think it's about us. How often do we leave on Sunday and say, "I didn't get anything out of today's

sermon?" Or, "The praise team keeps singing the same songs." Complaining because we aren't happy. The service didn't go our way. What about all the others in the room? Did we do more than shake hands and give trite greetings? Do we breathe in the words of the songs and let them flow out to God? When worship becomes all about us, we get bored.

3. Maybe we need to do something, and not eat a cardboard box. It's possible our spiritual lives are boring because we aren't doing anything. We expect God, or others, to do everything for us.

4. We seek entertainment or excitement rather than worship. Instead of entering the gates of worship expecting to give, we're ready to get. We tend to put nice words on it like "being fed." But we're adults; we don't need to be fed. We need to give—give ourselves to God.

Are we settling for cardboard boxes? Instead of experiencing the wonder of the Holy Spirit, we slump in our seat and kick aside what doesn't personally appeal. We look for what we think is the tasty morsels.

Maybe we need to make some changes in our ideas about worship. Think. Does that change begin with us? Like the Psalmist, we need to enter his gates giving thanks, not the expectation of what's in it for me.

Enter his gates with thanksgiving, and his courts with praise! Give thanks to him; bless his name!–Psalm 100:4

DONKEY SIZE

Have you ever seen a miniature donkey? They look like a stuffed, plush toy given to a child. The first time I encountered the tiny creatures I thought *How adorable.* My second thought was *What are these little guys used for?*

I was convinced the minis must be for show only. At one time, the miniature donkey, which originated in Italy, was used around the house to grind wheat at a mill in the house, carry water from the well, and to pack supplies to shepherds in the mountains. Today they are generally pets.

Most of us are familiar with a standard-size donkey. These are the ones often seen in pictures. When we think of riding a donkey, we picture an adult astride a short animal, feet nearly dragging the ground.

Some breeds of donkeys can measure taller than a standard horse—fourteen to fifteen hands (a "hand" is about four inches). When someone is riding one of these mammoth animals, they can appear to be riding a horse. A donkey can also be trained for shows, even performing events such as dressage, much like a horse.

In Bible times, royalty rode donkeys during times of peace. Entering a city on a donkey was a sign of peace. Can you picture the scene? A king, in all his finery, straddle a donkey with his feet nearly dragging the ground. Not a picture of authority, is it?

While we'd like to think royalty rode on mammoth donkeys, it wasn't possible. George Washington developed this breed. These tall animals can rival a Clydesdale in size. When groomed, the mammoths have the same luxurious coat as a horse.

Our standard-size Jeb can stand regally with his head held high. Yes, Jeb is also prideful. He'll give a look of "I'm in charge here."

Sometimes we think we're too small to be of value. Maybe we don't think of ourselves as cute as a mini donkey, and we sit by as though we can't do what the "big" guys do. We think only the mammoth donkey can do the heavy jobs, and we're not strong enough. The fact of the matter is the mammoth was bred for one reason—to be breeding stock for stronger mules. Unlike their tiny counterparts, the massive creatures aren't quite as useful in day-to-day business.

The same is true of us. We don't have to be "big" to be significant to the kingdom of God. We don't need to be important to have influence for the kingdom of God. Our society has made standing out a norm; anything else is unacceptable. Thankfully, we live in the kingdom of God where the minis are as important as the mammoth.

Humble yourselves, therefore, under the mighty hand of God so that at the proper time he may exalt you.—1 Peter 5:6

DISTRACTED BY GREEN GRASS

We move our donkeys to different pastures a couple times each year. They'll eat down one, so we take them where they can get more luscious grass while the other grows back.

It's not a hard task. Put the halter on the donkey, attach a rope lead, take a short walk to the other pasture. On occasion, the donkey will nibble at new delicacies found along the way, but primarily the stroll is pleasant.

Well, usually it's a pleasant stroll. For some reason, one particular jaunt to greener pastures was fraught with delays.

Neesy had only made this walk a couple times. Shortly after she moved in with us, we moved her from a pasture where she was alone to join Jeb in another. She seemed anxious to explore the new area and to meet her new pasture companion. But that's a whole other story. I was sure this trip would be the same.

This time, the five-minute walk turned into a thirty-minute struggle. Yes, even a battle of wills.

Neesy stopped every few steps to grab a snack. But the usual gentle tugs on the lead didn't get her moving again. When she did move, she would circle around to head back the other direction. No, she didn't want to go back the former abode. She wanted to go back to another delicacy.

I would get her moving in the correct direction for a few steps, and she'd stop to munch as though she hadn't ever seen green grass before. The battle of wills began again.

We are told donkeys are stubborn, but they are cautious. This time, I was sure Neesy had developed a stubborn streak. I knew she knew where she was going—to greener pastures. I knew she knew there was no danger in the route she had been over before. I knew she was behaving like a spoiled four-year-old.

I wasn't going to be bested by a spoiled donkey.

Unlike Balaam, I didn't beat Neesy with a rod. I don't hit our donks. But I tried to cajole her with treats. Nope. In her estimation, these weren't as good as whatever she found on the ground. I tried letting her take the lead for a few moments. Like that spoiled four-year-old, she took advantage of the tactic by wandering further from the path.

Needless to say, by the time we got through the gate of the new pasture. I was beyond annoyed. But we made it.

I'm reminded of how many times we're distracted by the greener grass. We clearly hear God's direction. We start out with him, then there it is—greener grass or a new plant. We turn aside and nibble. God cajoles, tugs, and sometimes stops us along the way.

Once we finally make our way to the pasture God had in mind for us, we're tired. We're amazed we finally got to our destination. All too often, we wonder why God didn't bring us straight to the new grass.

He tried. We thought we knew the best place to stop and eat. He rerouted us. We turned to go back. Sometimes he's even given us a treat to move us along to where he knows there is a better pasture, better grass, better food for us. We may think the donkey is stubborn. Really, we're the stubborn creatures.

We're easily distracted from God's best for a temporary, good morsel. We can be distracted by where we've been, which seems so comfortable. We're more comfortable in the known rather than moving to the unknown. Dare I say, we think we've arrived when we have a little morsel of a delicious treat.

God leads us directly to the green pasture, the best pasture, the way we should go. How much easier it would be if we would just follow?

He makes me lie down in green pastures.
—Psalms 23:2

DONKEYS AS A SYMBOL OF WEALTH

The old man slumps along the road. Rags to cover his body—none adequate against the blowing cold. He holds the frayed rope, which is wrapped around the beast of burden's neck. Moving is difficult for both of them.

Admit it. We often visualize the beast of burden as a donkey. I'm not sure where the image of a donkey being used only by the poor came from. A humble creature too lowly for anyone else.

In fact, when wealth is described in the Bible, donkeys (or as some versions say "ass") are listed. Read these descriptions:

- Genesis 25:35–Abraham's servant tells Rebekah God has given his master donkeys as part of his wealth.
- Numbers 31:4–The Israelites took 61,000 donkeys in the plunder from battle with the Midianites.
- Job 42:12–Among God's blessings after Job's trials were one thousand female donkeys.
- Exodus 20:17–We are even told not to covet our neighbors' donkeys in the Ten Commandments.

To have a large number of donkeys was an indication of a person's worth. "He's worth one thousand donkeys." Their value is further indicated by not only the fact donkeys are counted, they are also named in the list: cattle, sheep, donkeys. God considers them important enough to count.

What is it about a donkey that gives the impression of being for the poor and not the wealthy? Could it be their humble demeanor? Or the myths surrounding donkeys, such as being stubborn. Maybe the cartoons of a donkey being pulled along a road.

Today, a donkey is highly valued in some poorer parts of the world because of the work they do to support daily life by hauling, transportation, and production. The burdens of the donkey help put food on the table, carry children to school, and build better lives.

Our culture tends to look on outside appearances to judge value. A horse is nicer looking than a donkey—larger, sleeker, not such long ears. Thus, the horse is judged as more valuable. With some digging, we realize the value of donkeys.

We do the same thing with our fellow humans. We judge by appearance. Too often we have to dig to understand the value of some people. We've all heard stories of wealthy people disguising themselves as poor to learn how people live in the real world. We judge on the exterior alone.

The way someone looks means nothing to God. He tells us not to look on the outside. Jesus tells us not to judge by appearance (John 7:24). Paul reminds us we shouldn't boast about what is seen, but rather by the heart (2 Cor 5:12). Yes, we're human. We see the outside first.

We need to get to know others before deciding their value. God valued all people enough to have his Son die for their eternal souls. Can't we value them enough to look beyond the clothes, the face, or even the money?

But the Lord said to Samuel, "Do not look
on his appearance or on the height of his
stature, because I have rejected him. For
the Lord sees not as man sees: man looks on
the outward appearance, but the Lord looks
on the heart." –1 Samuel 16:7

ABOUT THE AUTHOR

Susan K. Stewart didn't grow up with aspirations of being a donkey whisperer. Her childhood dream was to be Lois Lane by day and a ballet dancer by night. She met her Superman, moved from the city to a mountain village, and began raising their family of superkids.

She grew up in a traveling family. (Susan went to fourteen different schools before graduating high school.) Of all the places her family lived, a rural ranch was not one of them. Pet donkeys and surly chickens were not part of Susan's life experience or her bucket list.

Then it happened. Susan met a donkey nose-to-muzzle and a special bond was created. After her first visit to the Peaceful Valley Donkey Rescue, Susan wanted donkey pets. Alas, their property was too small to meet the adoption requirements. When they made the move from California to Texas, donkeys soon became a part of the small ranch.

Susan and husband Bob raised their three children in the mountains of Central California. All three of the kids graduated from their homeschool and, now with families of their own, live in different states. Susan and Bob have the six smartest and most beautiful grandchildren God could bless them with.

In 2010, Susan and Bob packed all of their worldly processions, along with two dogs and two cats, and moved to cattle ranchland of Central Texas. Here they tend three cats, three dogs, an unruly flock of chickens, and two surly and wonderful donkeys.

Susan is a writer and editor. She has written four books including the award-winning *Formatting e-Books for Writers*. When she's not walking and conversing with her donkeys, Susan tends her vegetable garden, tracks family history, and reads everything from the great American novel to the back of cereal boxes.

CONNECT WITH SUSAN:

Website: http://www.practicalinspirations.com
Facebook: https://www.facebook.com/susan.k.stewart/
https://www.facebook.com/DonkeyDevo
Pinterest: https://www.pinterest.com/susankstewart/donkey-whispers/
Twitter: https://twitter.com/susan_stewart

DONKEY WHISPERS

Get monthly doses of wisdom from Jeb, Nessy, and their friends. Sign-up now and receive a devotion not included in this book. https://www.susankstewart.com/freedonkeydevo

ENDNOTES

1. Dror Ben Ami. 2012. "Torah Metaphors: The Donkey in Scripture." *The Time of Israel.* November 6, 2012. https://blogs.timesofisrael.com/torah-metaphors-the-donkey-in-Scripture

2. Julia Attaway. "What Does 'Let Go' and 'Let God' Really Mean?" *Guideposts.* https://www.guideposts.org/inspiration/inspiring-stories/stories-of-faith/what-does-let-go-and-let-god-really-mean

DONKEY RESCUE RESOURCES

AN INCOMPLETE LIST OF DONKEY RESCUES

As you've read, a spur-of-the-moment visit to Peaceful Valley Donkey Rescue ignited my passion for the misunderstood and often unloved donkey. I have admiration for the many people, who out of kindness and a caring spirit, rescue and care for thousands of donkeys around the world. I've included a few of the rescues I've had contact with over the years. Each quarter a portion of the proceeds from this book will be donated to one of these organizations.

A trip around the United States visiting donkey rescues is on my bucket list. I encourage you to visit a rescue near you and become acquainted with the gentle animals. Trust me, your life will be changed. To learn more about donkeys and where you can visit a rescue, go to Donkey Wise, www. donkeywise.org.

PEACEFUL VALLEY DONKEY RESCUE (TEXAS)

Mark and Amy Meyers started the Peaceful Valley Donkey Rescue as a backyard hobby more than a decade ago. After purchasing their first donkey Izzy as a pet, the Meyers began to notice other donkeys in their community in various stages of abuse and neglect. Not knowing exactly what to do, Amy began buying up these donkeys and Mark spent his evenings talking to the donkeys and fixing their various ailments. It was after the twenty-fifth donkey came into the Meyers's home they decided to open an actual rescue so they would be able to find safe, loving homes for their donkeys.

This simple gesture of love has turned into the largest rescue of its kind. The Meyers still stay involved in the day-to-day operations of the rescue, but they also manage a large staff to ensure the well-being of the more than 3,000 donkeys under their direct care.

Under the Meyers's direction, Peaceful Valley has grown to the largest rescue of its kind with facilities all across the United States.

https://donkeyrescue.org/

HEALING HEARTS DONKEY SHELTER AND RESCUE (WASHINGTON)

Healing Hearts' mission is threefold: to provide a safe haven for abandoned, neglected, abused and unwanted donkeys while providing training and rehabilitation to help them find a loving, nurturing, forever home; to provide a safety net where adoptable donkeys whose owners, for whatever reason, find themselves in a position where they can no longer keep them but want to be assured that their beloved donkeys do not end up in an abusive or neglectful home, at an auction, or shipped off to a slaughter house; and to educate the public and donkey owners to form a better understanding of donkeys and their needs.

Healing Hearts also serves as a Satellite Adoption Center for Peaceful Valley Donkey Rescue, the largest donkey rescue in our nation.

https://hhdonkey.org

LONGHOPES DONKEY SHELTER (COLORADO)

The Longhopes Donkey Shelter was incorporated January 2000 but began in 1998 when the founder, Kathy Dean, went looking for her own donkeys. She knew there were unwanted donkeys needing homes, but she was unable to find them, because unwanted donkeys were usually sold for slaughter at local sale barns. Wanting to offer an alternative, Kathy learned that rescuing donkeys was impossible without a facility where the donkeys could be rehabilitated and trained until a new owner was found.

In August 1999, Kathy and her husband Alan Miller bought twenty acres in Bennett. That month, Kathy took in Rocky, a 42-year-old donkey whose owner could no longer keep him. By January 2000, Kathy had nine donkeys. That was when Kathy decided to formalize her passion and create an equine shelter to serve donkeys in the Rocky Mountains.

https://longhopes.org/

LITTLE LONGEARS MINIATURE DONKEY RESCUE (MARYLAND)

Little Longears is dedicated to the rescue, rehabilitation, and safe sanctuary of abused, neglected, or otherwise unwanted donkeys. They also provide a safe haven for owners to surrender their donkeys in the event they are no longer able to care for them. After veterinary, farrier, psychological, and training needs are met, their goal is to place adoptable donkeys into permanent, loving homes as appropriate, or to provide permanent sanctuary as needed.

https://www.littlelongears.org/

T & D DONKEY RESCUE (MISSOURI)

T & D is dedicated to at-risk, neglected, abandoned, and abused donkeys. They provide each with medical attention to address any immediate physical needs, ongoing veterinary care, and farrier care. If a donkey cannot be rehabilitated, physically or psychologically, they will live at the rescue as long as they are comfortably able. Working closely with veterinarians, equine chiropractor, and farriers, decisions are based on what is best for every donkey and the rescue. The donkeys live in herds in a natural environment. While adoption is not the main focus, select donkeys are available for adoption under contract to the right home. By providing educational opportunities to increase awareness of the horrific conditions many donkeys endure, as well as the specific needs of donkeys, T & D strives to reduce future cruelties through this awareness.

https://www.tddonkeyrescueinc.org/

TURNING POINTE DONKEY RESCUE (MICHIGAN)

Turning Pointe Donkey Rescue (aka TPDR and/or the rescue) is a Michigan-based nonprofit organization dedicated to the health and welfare of miniature, standard, and mammoth donkeys.

Through the rescue, humane care and proper training of these *long ears* is promoted. TPDR strives to provide the public with a better understanding of their true nature.

Their efforts are directed towards education of perspective and current donkey owners. Donkeys come to the rescue from a variety of difficult situations. They are matched with the most compatible, compassionate, and supportive environment.

https://turningpointedonkeyrescue.com/

LUCKY A RANCH (ARIZONA)

A nonprofit public charity located in the White Mountains of Arizona, Lucky A Ranch provides a safe landing for donkeys and mules in need. The ranch takes in animals that have been left behind due to no fault of their own. Neglected, abused, and unwanted donkeys are welcomed.

Lucky A is also home to the rare breed of the Poitou donkeys. They are part of helping bring the breed back. The have one jack Poitou and several jennies and are hoping for some offspring.

https://luckyaranch.org/

ZEN DONKEY SANCTUARY (ARIZONA)

Zen Donkey Sanctuary, Inc. is a 501(c)(3) charitable organization committed to providing compassionate care to abused, abandoned, neglected, sick, or injured at risk donkeys by providing a safe, loving, and nurturing environment for healing and restoration. The primary goal is to rescue, rehabilitate, and to rehome the animals in their care. Those animals not appropriate for adoption will live out their lives at the sanctuary with love and dignity.

https://www.zendonkey.org/

Made in the USA
Las Vegas, NV
14 January 2024

84359289R00085